Called to Womanhood

Focal Point Series

ReViewing the Movies:
A Christian Response to Contemporary Film
by Peter Fraser and Vernon Edwin Neal

Christians in a .com World:
Getting Connected Without Getting Consumed
by Gene Edward Veith, Jr. and Chris Stamper

Called to Womanhood:
A Biblical View for Today's World
by Beth Impson

FOCAL POINT SERIES

Gene Edward Veith, Jr., general editor

Called to Womanhood

A Biblical View for Today's World

Beth Impson

CROSSWAY BOOKS • WHEATON, ILLINOIS
A DIVISION OF GOOD NEWS PUBLISHERS

Called to Womanhood: A Biblical View for Today's World

Copyright © 2001 by Beth Impson

Published by Crossway Books
a division of Good News Publishers
1300 Crescent Street
Wheaton, Illinois 60187

Cover design: David LaPlaca

Cover photo: PhotoDisc™

First printing 2001

Printed in the United States of America

Library of Congress Cataloging-in-Publication Data
Impson, Beth, 1952–
    Called to womanhood : a biblical view for today's world / Beth Impson.
       p. cm. — (Focal point series)
    Includes biographical references and index.
    ISBN 1-58134-262-4 (pbk. : alk. paper)
    1. Christian women—Religious life. I. Title. II. Series.
BV4527.I48 2001
248.8'43—dc21
                                      2001001916
                                            CIP

15	14	13	12	11	10	09	08	07	06	05	04	03	02	01
15	14	13	12	11	10	9	8	7	6	5	4	3	2	1

To Mother
always my example of godly womanhood

and Daddy
who has never failed to love his little girl

Contents

Acknowledgments

The image of the writer in his lonely garret may present a romantic, bohemian idea of the profession. But no writing comes to publication without the involvement of many, many others. I have been blessed all my life with the encouragement of people who believed in and challenged me, who have not allowed me to hide this ability beneath the bushels of busyness or laziness or fear of criticism. Blessings to you all, especially:

Saints I've never met in person but who prayed for me, discussed issues with me, sent me resources, helped me to think clearly: Bill Mouser of the International Center for Gender Studies, the many participants in the Complementarian Christian Coalition (especially Dr. Nick Beadles), those who run the web site of the Council for Biblical Manhood and Womanhood, and those I've met through other interests I pursue on the Web (Eric, Heather, Don W., Don D., Dave P., Ken—RCJH!)—thank you for helping me keep perspective and persevere, each in your unique way.

My colleagues and the administration and staff of Bryan College: how can I ever thank all of you, or thank any of you enough? Steve Bradshaw and Jim Coffield—thanks for sharing so many of your resources and so much of your time. Ray Legg and Whit Jones—thanks for understanding my craziness and allowing me less departmental responsibility while in the midst of this project. David and Barbara Masoner—your prayers and loving concern have encouraged me daily. Marcy Froemke—

how could I have done this without the many discussions of writing with a kindred spirit? Vonnie Johnson and Laura Kaufman—your help with library resources, especially in the wake of the building fire that left us all in desperate straits, went beyond the call of duty and saved me from weeks of new research and writing. Many others have prayed regularly and offered encouragement in various ways—may God richly repay you all.

My students: your prayers, your patience, your discussion, your questions and genuine interest—you teach me in so many ways and provide motivation for me to keep learning. And our discussions of this topic give me hope that feminism has not yet blinded your entire generation; may you joyfully embrace God's calling on you, particularly in the vocation of manhood or womanhood God has given you.

The wonderful staff at Crossway: you have all been so gracious walking this neophyte through her first book publication, and you have made it so painless. Special thanks to Jill Carter for answers to a hundred questions and to Ted Griffin for making the manuscript clearer and better while retaining not just my meaning but my voice.

Ed Veith: I would never have written *this* book had you not asked me to, and I am deeply grateful for the opportunity. Thanks for your guidance and your encouragement throughout the process, and your gracious challenges to both my thinking and my writing style, all of which have made the book—and everything else I've written since that first book review for *World*—far better than I would have thought possible.

Jim Hartman: I can't remember not writing, but the road to publication began during finals week of my first semester at the University of Kansas, when the most demanding teacher I've ever had said to me, "Keep writing; you've got what it takes."

Thank you, Jim, for giving me what I needed of both skill and confidence to know that my dreams could someday be within my reach.

Cindy, Jenny, Dana, and Mollie: I couldn't have completed this project without your prayers, but your love has meant so much more in my life. You know whereof I speak.

This book is dedicated to my parents: I am so privileged to be your daughter. Thank you for your never-wavering belief in me. And Michael, my big brother—you're the best.

My children: Joshua, David, Davina, Sarah—I appreciate your prayers and encouragement in the midst of the separate and busy lives you now lead. I am delighted to be your mom. And Daniel—what a trooper you've been! Thanks, buddy, for the hugs and the drawings and the prayers and the patience—and for being my daily reminder that the most important thing was never the book.

Keiller: your patience has been extraordinary as I've hogged the computer, talked incessantly about feminism, spent a small fortune on paper and ink cartridges, and generally been even more distracted than usual. I am privileged and honored to be loved by you.

Finally, without the Lord Jesus, I could do nothing worth the doing. I only pray that the work here glorifies Him—nothing else matters.

CHAPTER ONE

"Let Her Works Praise Her"

§

My mother has spent her adulthood as a full-time home-maker, and, although my own role as sole wage-earner for my family differs in its daily round, still the example of her life guides me. Only as I have had to grapple with this role, one I would never have voluntarily chosen, have I come to under-stand womanhood itself as a calling, one that can be fulfilled in any circumstances God allows. And while I see my mother's womanhood lived out in the details of her domestic activities, it is the principles by which she lives that ultimately teach and inspire me. Thus, since womanhood is the subject of this book, and since she is my daily example of the richness and fullness of life a woman can enjoy, it seems fitting to begin with her portrait.

The last summer that both my parents were in their seven-ties, they drove two days from Austin to our home in Tennessee, stayed here a day, then drove us to Virginia for our oldest son's wedding. During the one day they "rested" at our house, my mother spent almost as much time in the kitchen as I did. "You don't have to wash the dishes," I would say.

"I have to do *something*," would be her reply as she reached for the detergent.

I cannot remember my mother not doing something. In fact, as harried and exhausted and overworked as I often feel, my mother's energy and accomplishments still put me to shame, even as she approaches her eightieth birthday. Yet hers is not a doing out of mere duty or obligation, a Martha-like whirl that neglects the "one thing [that] is needed." Rather, she engages in constant service to her Lord and to those He has brought into her life to love and honor and cherish, in whatever way her hands have found.

My mother has shown me all my life what it means to be a woman, to embrace womanhood as a calling and to live it out in every interaction. Her being a homemaker does not mean I am suggesting that women are to be like some of the TV home-makers of the fifties, idealized women who made idols of home and family as surely as today's media make idols of careers and worldly success. Rather, in telling my mother's story I wish to share a portrait of a woman who puts neither family nor "self-fulfillment" in the place of God, but lives in joyful service to those placed closest to her—family always being first—because this is God's call on her life, her service to Him above all. She models for me the Proverbs 31 woman, and I am proud to "rise up and call her blessed."

What makes the Proverbs 31 woman "excellent" (v. 10, NASB)? Her industriousness, her prudence, her compassion; her joy and contentment; above all, her godliness. In considering these qualities, images of my mother abound. Not that she is perfect; she would be the first to protest such a description. Yet her particular frailties honestly tend to escape me, for they pale beside the achievements of her life. Certainly I was blessed to grow up in a time when married women commonly stayed at home, and to be raised in a home where my mother could devote herself to her family. I have the impression that all important conversations with my mother have taken place in the common rounds of domesticity—at the sewing machine putting in zippers or ripping out seams, or in the kitchen chopping vegetables or washing dishes.

I learned from my mother that to enjoy the fruits of one's labor, one must labor—and with diligence. If the house were to be healthy and welcoming, to family as well as friends, someone had to clean it; and so I did nothing on Saturdays until I had helped dust and vacuum and had made my own room presentable. If a nutritious and attractive meal were to appear at supper time, the ingredients had to be on hand, the meat taken out in time to thaw, homemade rolls or cornbread started at the right moment to be hot on the table. And I became a part of all such preparations from a very early age.

Even when we left early on a fall morning for Kansas City to spend the day shopping at the Plaza, Mother knew what we would have for supper and made any advance preparations necessary. She organized her mind within the daily routine of a family, and her skill and efficiency allowed for productive time with her husband and each of us children, as well as numerous projects to benefit family, friends, and strangers. Such a way of life means no time for empty hands. "Now, Bess," my father often says, "why don't you just sit down and relax for a while?" "As soon as I finish . . ." is her most frequent reply. And when she does join us for conversation, needlework or mending occupies her hands; in front of the television, she will be sewing or ironing or reading. Perhaps the oddest sight in our home has always been several people in front of a television program, all with their noses stuck in books or magazines. My love of books and knowledge comes from the example of both my parents.

The loving respect of my parents for each other has greatly shaped my attitude toward marriage. There is no doubt that my father is the "head of the house," but my mother is his full partner. They work out all major decisions together, but she readily and naturally defers to his preferences—say, about how long a visit to "the kids" will last or where to eat out. It's not because she "ought" to; it's just her heart attitude of valuing others more than herself and finding pleasure in their happiness. Nor does she hesitate to point out some foolishness in him. It's part of the partnership, after all, to hold each other accountable. It seems to me this understanding has always been comfortable, and part of that has been my mother's availability to make a home—healthy meals, attractive decor, order and harmony, all within the means provided by my father's work.

An old proverb says, "He that will thrive must ask his wife leave." I have known women who drained a husband's excellent income through a lack of wisdom and prudence, buying what they could make or do without. My family always had enough, but even in the days of real plenty, my mother has acted prudently with money and goods. My parents' ability to travel today has as much to do with the economy she practiced every day over the past fifty-plus years as with the income my father earned.

Growing up, I recall an occasional Sunday noon trip to Griff's for ten-cent hamburgers as a rare and exciting treat, or perhaps an A&W root beer float on a hot summer evening. Those trips to the Plaza? Mostly window-shopping as we kept a sharp eye out for ideas for clothing or decorations or gifts we could make. Each rare trip had two highlights—a fancy lunch at Macy's or Putsch's cafeteria or the little French restaurant nearby, and our visit to Hancock's, where we began our hunt for the classiest patterns—my mother's skill allowing us to mix and match the features we liked from several—and for the prettiest and most durable fabrics to make them with. Even today, with no time to sew my own clothes, I find it hard to pay the necessary price for high quality; in the back of my mind, my mother's voice whispers, "We could make that for so much less."

Among my first memories, I see myself on the floor in my mother's sewing area, a box open before me, in my hands a thread heavy with every style of button imaginable. When she began to let me use the old black Singer that my daughters now have, she sat beside me, her hands guiding mine until I learned to hold the material straight and exactly tight enough to guide without forcing it, avoiding the needle that could so easily pierce my small fingers. At the kitchen table, covered with a sewing mat, she taught me how to pin and cut a pattern, using the least amount of material possible to have enough left over for a belt or scarf or other accessory. She made me pull the material each way to feel it give on the bias and hold on the straight, explaining the difference and its importance in laying out the pattern.

She taught me, too, when to follow directions precisely and when a shortcut actually saves time. You can clip the notches on the pattern, for example, instead of cutting out around them, as long as the clip stays within the seam width. Basting a seam before machine-sewing it is optional too, if you pin it straight; it takes a bit more care while sewing to avoid breaking the needle on one of the pins but saves far more time in the long run. On the other hand, the pattern has to be laid precisely on the fabric if you want it to hang properly in the finished garment, and a curved seam has to be clipped to fit well and to avoid tearing out—but you never clip until you're sure the seam is right.

In the kitchen, too, she taught me the essentials and the options. Sifting flour isn't necessary if you scoop just so much from the cup before adding it to the bowl, and a host of substitutes allow for pleasing variety (and cabinets empty of some called-for ingredient). But margarine and shortening yield very different products, and woe to the cook who forgets the difference between baking soda and baking powder. And always, whether at the sewing machine or the kitchen counter, presentation holds as much value as quality. Lace or embroidery or a ruffle creates beauty and a unique garment. Apple slices and orange sections are never thrown into a bowl but are arranged artistically on a plate; no pots or pans sit on her table, but rather attractive serving dishes; and a clean tablecloth and often flowers or some pleasant ornament complete an atmosphere that honors those who share the meal, with family as cherished as guests.

And even as my mother taught me by example to pursue excellence and to value family and friends, she taught me by example to value those who are different and to have compassion for those who are needy. Our family's participation in the University of Kansas host family program exposed me to people of different nations and cultures. The prejudiced remarks of some of my friends shocked me when, early in high school, I brought a black friend home for dinner—I hadn't realized that real people felt that way about skin color. Having vegetarians from the Middle East for Thanksgiving dinner, ironing the over-curly hair of a young Turkish woman, hosting a strong-willed German girl for a year on the American Field Service program—these experiences shaped my attitudes toward people, building understanding and empathy and respect.

Though less aware of my mother's work for the needy in our community, I remember helping her make and distribute Thanksgiving and Christmas baskets, and I remember her volunteer work distributing food and clothing in a poor neighborhood, work she still does today. Perhaps because her grandmother raised her, my mother has always had a special affection for the elderly as well. Among the most vivid images from my youth are visits to Gracie in her small, not-too-well-maintained home in North Lawrence, my mother carefully braiding the diminutive woman's white, nearly knee-length hair, winding the braids about her head, then bringing her to our home for her favorite lunch of cornmeal mush. And even after my grandfather died, having lived in the Valley View rest home for a year or so, Mother continued her visits to residents she had met on her daily visits to him, some of whom had no other visitors.

I remember also the friends she fellowshipped with, the church activities, her ferrying my brother and me to our many activities until we could drive, listening to us, encouraging us, teaching us life lessons and challenging our rebellions. Letters flowed from her pen every Sunday afternoon. Creative projects for the church bazaar or gifts for the decoration of our home busied her hours too, along with such occasional projects as Santa's Cookie Tree (our Christmas gift to the neighborhood), helping my father plan and build our country house, and sponsoring the Christian women's club I belonged to in college.

It never occurred to me to wonder if my mother was enjoying this life so wrapped up in her family and community. And I don't wonder about it now; I don't need to ask her. Her every day radiates contentment and joy, a genuinely fulfilled life. She does not trumpet her faith in many words, but it undergirds all that she is and does, and her contentment tells me more clearly than her words ever could that she lives the life of servanthood to which Jesus calls each of us.

I wanted nothing more in my own life than to be like my mother. I married a man who planned to support our family without extra income from me, and I intended to make a peaceful, creative, contented home for him and our children. I'll readily admit that the first few years of marriage were far more stormy than peaceful, as two strong wills clashed and I hadn't yet understood the foundation of my mother's success—putting others first. Then, just as I began to catch a glimpse of my failings, circumstances crumbled my dreams.

Forcing me into being the sole wage earner for our family (then four children, later five), God gave me a new challenge: to learn contentment in circumstances I would never have chosen. Having fought that lesson in the circumstances I'd always wanted, I was ill-prepared, but over the years I find that my mother's example still illuminates the right path.

Slowly I have come to understand that life for me, as for my mother, is still about being a woman. This identity is the most basic to my existence. I am, of course, a wife and mother because I am a woman (I cannot be husband or father), though these are not essential to being a woman. My teaching and my writing are informed by my womanhood—not merely my experiences as a woman, but my very perspectives and ways of thinking and reacting. My friendships take on the qualities they do because I am a woman. And for me, as for my mother, my identity as a woman takes on special meaning because I understand that it is no accident. God created me a woman, with a special purpose and a special place dependent on that identity. This is where I must begin in my search for how to live in circumstances so opposed to my dreams and desires.

Growing up in an era where "feminists" seemed easy to dismiss (the only ones I heard about were the bra-burning men-haters), I had to find myself caught in circumstances foreign to my childhood models and dreams before I gave serious consideration to what this identity of "woman" is all about. From my childhood perspective it simply meant being a wife and mother, and I couldn't understand the fuss some women seemed to make about it. I suppose I hardly gave a thought to single women, and I had seen no examples of the genuine problems many women face that might have challenged my simplistic notions. But when my own roles in life became more complex and complicated, when I felt myself torn between home and work and writing and was at times resentful of God, at times of men, at times of other women, I came to see that I needed more than simplistic answers, no matter who was giving them.

Reading Tillie Olson's *Silences* shocked me from my complacency and avoidance. Here was a woman with a tremendous gift of language, who loved her children and wanted to give to them the way my mother had given to me, yet struggled with the demands of providing even basic physical care, much less emotional nurture, in the midst of real poverty, with the concurrent desire and need to use her gift of writing. Without the bitterness that I had sensed in other feminist writers, she simply said that the very act of living sometimes silences us, and she wondered how to live with dreams that can't come true. As the margins of her book began to fill with my "yes!" again and again, I knew it was time to go before God and find out who He desires me to be and how I am to live that out in my particular circumstances and in a world increasingly hostile to Him and to His servants.

So as I put this book together, praying that my answers would not become glib or simplistic, but reflect the wisdom of the One who created me a woman and placed me where He desires me to wholeheartedly serve Him, my mother's example continues to light the way. Her embracing of and contentment in the vocation of womanhood remind me every moment of the gift He has given in making me her daughter, with the opportunity to honor her through imitation of her attitudes and character though our circumstances differ.

The book follows my own journey to a large degree. Understanding early feminism and the genuine problems of women in a very different culture from our modern one helped me place the feminist movement in context and develop a better sensitivity to the very real problems feminists identify for us if we will listen. Yet today's feminism, at least that radical brand of it that most of us identify with the term, is very different—confusing, perhaps frightening to some. Undoubtedly, some who call themselves feminists value home and family, but they are not the "feminists" who influence the culture, not by a long shot. Today's feminism is so radical (and even some who are less radical clearly accept the premises of the radical feminists) that no matter how passionate I might be about women's issues, I cannot call myself a feminist. Nevertheless, seeing how cultural, social, and worldview changes have brought about the new feminism has helped me to understand its pervasiveness in the twenty-first century.

I have found that feminists in the church, while goodwilled in their efforts to seek a biblical solution to the problems facing women today, primarily offer the same answers as the world's feminists, with a scriptural veneer. The influence of the media and the pervasiveness of relativistic and modern feminist assumptions in the culture are hard to shake off. Yet many women today who are seeking fulfillment already know that the world offers only emptiness. If the church offers nothing better, nothing different, we do them great injury. I hope to lovingly suggest that my sisters can better help those who struggle by facing the clear meaning of Scripture and helping us to see how it doesn't imprison us but frees us to be the women God created us to be. Most, though not all, by God's design, will marry and have children. Whatever their situation, whether they work outside the home or not, their family will be their primary focus.

They have, however, been gulled into thinking that the home life is dull and demeaning. I hope to show this lie for what it is, and to present God's superior alternative.

In the chapters on our relationships to men, to children, to the work world, and to the church, I will remember that not all women are married and that not all women enjoy every aspect of what is traditionally considered "women's work." Though we are all women, we are individuals as well, and our gifts, talents, and particular circumstances will make our outward roles varied, though always based in the identity of woman given by God at conception. I hope to show that the biblical constraints given to women are not meant to shackle or deprive us, any more than are constraints given to men or to children, but rather to guide us to the areas of our greatest ministry and influence, where we can be the most free to take God's message to a lost world.

My final emphasis will be on the value of this vocation, this womanhood, in God's eyes. Ultimately each woman stands or falls before God, not before men. In prayerful submission to Scripture, we must make every decision to glorify Him, not to please men or to fulfill personal desires. "*I* will give you the desires of your heart," He tells us. In pleasing Him by embracing the identity He has given us, we become salt and light in a world gone amok, a world that seems to have lost all sense of direction, all sense of values. We can be the servants He commands every believer to be, drawing others to Him through our own relationship with Him. And we can be fulfilled *as women—* only and fully—in following His direction for our lives.

CHAPTER TWO

Early Feminism: Sowing the Seeds

§

As we all know, even women in the western world have not always had the freedoms and opportunities we have today. What little education most eighteenth- and nineteenth-century middle- and upper-class women received was not intellectual in nature but was rather preparation for the game of wealthy husband hunting. An unmarried woman might have been able to teach as a governess or a schoolmarm, but college attendance or pursuit of any other career was most rare. Many women wrote—a vocation that could be followed in the privacy of the home; but those who desired to write serious literature or non-fiction often chose a male pseudonym in order to be taken seriously by the intellectual elite (mostly men) of the day.

But even women who did not care to pursue higher education or careers lacked legal rights that we take for granted today. Besides not being allowed to vote, upon marriage a woman's property came under the sole ownership of her husband, any wages she might earn belonged to him solely, she could not testify in her own defense in court, she could not pursue divorce (even in cases of cruelty and abuse), and if her husband divorced her or she abandoned him, the children automatically were given into his custody, no matter what the circumstances. Inheritance laws left more to a son than to a surviving widow; often the widow could not even directly use anything left to her except through a male executor. The call for women's suffrage, then, was a call for involvement in the legal and social issues that directly and often negatively affected the women of the day.

Thus, the concerns of the early English and American feminists (though this term was not used until the modern movement) centered in political, legal, educational, and occupational equality for women, with goals that would protect women from unscrupulous husbands, lovers, or employers and allow them the freedom to develop all aspects of their humanity. These goals came from clearly identifiable cultural problems, and the feminists offered just as clear—and achievable—solutions for those problems. And in fact the goals of those early feminists have been largely, if not completely, met.

Understanding these issues and women's perspectives on them has helped me understand both the modern feminist movement and my own mixed responses to feminism. I certainly find that I have much more in common with these early feminists than with almost anyone who claims the name today. Yet the philosophical basis of even the early movement is, sadly, flawed in ways that have finally destroyed its rationality. In fact, many of the same false assumptions made by feminists today—both secular and in the church—formed the basis of early feminism as well, as we shall see.

The status and roles of women have of course varied throughout history and from place to place. In medieval times and into the Renaissance era, women could be found in many arenas—as business owners, shopkeepers, innkeepers, midwives (and even a rare doctor or two), writers, printers, perfume makers, fashion designers . . . And of course farm women had few moments to relax, what with feeding and clothing their own families as well as, often, running cottage industries and selling extra produce.

However, as upper-class mores crept into an increasing—and increasingly wealthy—middle class made up of tradesmen, and as industrialization began to change the entire face of the country, attitudes toward women and their status in society changed significantly. Just as middle-class folk became self-conscious about their speech, trying to talk like their social "betters" in order to be accepted by them, they imitated other signs of wealth. As Dorothy Sayers puts it, "The boast, 'My wife doesn't need to soil her hands with work,' first became general when the commercial middle classes acquired the plutocratic and aristocratic notion that the keeping of an idle woman was a badge of superior social status" (120 [citations throughout give page numbers for sources listed in "Works Cited" at the end of this book]). This led them to raise their daughters to concentrate on activities and attitudes that might "catch" a wealthy husband, perhaps even a "gentleman" (in the old-fashioned sense of a man with inherited property who didn't have to work).

Mrs. Bennet, in Jane Austen's novel *Pride and Prejudice*, epitomizes the typical middle- and upper-class woman of the late eighteenth and nineteenth centuries. Her only care in life is to see her five daughters "married well"—i.e., to men of means and connection, never mind their character. Her mind is filled with schemes and scandals, fashion and fancy. Her long-suffering husband is little better, letting her have her way in all things merely to keep peace and, in the process, allowing his daughters to be raised in the same foolish manner. Of their marriage Austen writes, "[Mr. Bennet], captivated by youth and beauty, and that appearance of good humour which youth and beauty generally give, had married a woman whose weak understanding and illiberal mind had very early in their marriage put an end to all real affection for her. Respect, esteem, and confidence had vanished for ever." Since, however, he was not a man given to vice, he consoled himself with hunting and reading; "to his wife he was very little otherwise indebted, than as her ignorance and folly had contributed to his amusement." This, of course, leads the children to have contempt for her as well (198).

When sixteen-year-old Lydia runs away with a soldier, Elizabeth says to their aunt, "[Lydia] has never been taught to think on serious subjects; and for the last half-year, nay, for a twelve-month, she has been given up to nothing but amusement and vanity. She has been allowed to dispose of her time in the most idle and frivolous manner, and to adopt any opinion that came in her way. Since the [militia] were first quartered in Meryton, nothing but love, flirtation, and officers have been in her head. She had been doing every thing in her power by thinking and talking on the subject, to give greater . . . susceptibility to her feelings; which are naturally lively enough" (236).

Austen is merely showing her readers what philosophical writers like Mary Wollstonecraft tell them. In her 1792 *A Vindication of the Rights of Woman*, Wollstonecraft condemns the education of middle- and upper-class women that leads to their emphasis on fashion and frippery, on wiles to catch a husband. "Men complain," she writes, "and with reason, of the follies and caprices of our sex, when they do not keenly satirize our headstrong passions and groveling vices.—Behold, I should answer, the natural effect of ignorance!" (19).

Women are treated as though they have no reason, Wollstonecraft complains. Men have claimed that woman's only purpose is to "please" them and thus have advocated and inculcated an educational system (if it can be called a system, as, she says, it has little order to it) that focuses attention on "pleasing" characteristics: agreeability, "accomplishments," fashion . . . Women "spend many of the first years of their lives acquiring a smattering of accomplishments; meanwhile strength of body and mind are sacrificed to libertine notions of beauty, to the desire of establishing themselves,—the only way women can rise in the world,—by marriage" (10).

At about the same time in the U.S., Judith Sargent Murray (writing under the pen name "Constantia") points out that if women are taught nothing but the domestic arts, they have no means to reason, no ability to form good judgment. Like Wollstonecraft, Murray doesn't advocate taking women away from domestic duties; she only notes that these alone cannot furnish material enough to satisfy an inquiring mind. "Is it reasonable," she asks, "that a candidate for immortality, for the joys of heaven, an intelligent being, who is to spend eternity contemplating the works of Deity, should at present be so degraded, as to be allowed no other ideas, than those which are suggested by the mechanism of a pudding, or sewing the seams of a garment?" (34).

Murray describes in general terms the education given American women of her day, a pattern Wollstonecraft implies as common for British women as well. For their first fifteen years, girls are strictly limited in their activities and are given "employments and recreations" that "enervate the body and debilitate the mind"; they are adorned from infancy with ribbons and other frills, so that they believe clothing to be the most important occupation of a woman's mind. Then at fifteen they are "introduced to the praise and adoration [flattery] of the world" and are taught how to be manipulative and cunning to get their way with men (Murray, 35-36). However, if they commit the least indiscretion of behavior, they are censured for not being stronger.

Murray draws the sensible conclusion, then, that perhaps if women were educated to have strong minds, they would behave better. (As Wollstonecraft puts it, "Complicated rules to adjust behaviour are a weak substitute for simple principles" [23].) Their youth, Murray says, could easily be spent in cultivation of the mind; then when their hands are busy with domestic duties, their minds will have material of substance for reflection. In fact, women have more time for study and reflection than men, because men's occupations generally require more mental attention.

Wollstonecraft explores the evils of this "education" of women in depth and attributes to it many of the ills of her society. Because women are only to be "pleasing" to men, the married woman will soon find that her charms, when on regular display, pall on her husband, who is then likely to look elsewhere for what he no longer sees in his wife. She cannot keep him from straying because she hasn't the intellectual ability to be a true friend and companion to him after his first infatuation wanes. And "faithless husbands make faithless wives," Wollstonecraft warns, as disappointed and angry women can hardly be blamed for using the only weapon at their disposal—their charm—to retaliate (6).

Women without intellectual development also make poor mothers, Wollstonecraft says. They have been raised to constrain their behavior, but not their emotions; in fact, they are taught to rely on their emotions almost exclusively. Thus, when faced with the necessity of overriding emotion in order to act from duty, such as rebuking or disciplining a child, they will be unable to do so and thus spoil their children. When they do rebuke a child, it will most likely be from the anger of the moment and thus inconsistent, so that the child cannot learn principles of good behavior. Such women will also tend to neglect their children for their own selfish desires, refusing to nurse them in order to save their figures and hiring others to teach and tend to them in order to have time for dressing and visiting.

Cunningness and manipulation are also a hallmark of weak intellect that women display. This is always how the weak have tyrannized over the strong, Wollstonecraft points out, and women will do so as long as men consider themselves superior merely because they have greater physical strength. Such women may well hold to the outward forms of propriety demanded by the society while making those around them miserable with their selfishness, perhaps even committing gross immoralities while appearing to be faithful wives.

Wollstonecraft also attacks the kind of "gallantry" that makes men pick up women's handkerchiefs or open doors or "protect" them from mice—when that gallantry is mere flattery and a statement of women's inferiority. She would rather see women not act like simpering idiots and do what they can for themselves, thus earning respect instead of false adulation for foolish sentiment and weakness. Men as well as women, she says, must become more chaste and modest in their behavior if society is to improve.

The result of this education in vanity is women who "are only anxious to inspire love [i.e., infatuation], when they ought to cherish a nobler ambition, and by their abilities and virtues exact respect" (7). Wollstonecraft's greatest goal for women is that they should "unfold their own faculties and acquire the dignity of conscious virtue" (26). And when we read the descriptions of the absurdity of so many women of the time, whether in novels like Austen's or treatises like Wollstonecraft's, it seems surprising that they allowed themselves to act this way. Yet women were not generally educated in the principles of reason and virtue, only the power of charm. And after all, most of us might be vain and lazy enough to enjoy unmerited attention and hope for nothing to do beyond deciding whether to have the cook prepare fish or veal for supper and who to place beside whom at the dinner party. The problem, of course, is that an empty mind and idle hands cannot provide the means to contentment over the long years of marriage that follow the triumphant "catch." Only a decent education and a shift in perspective could solve this problem. Wollstonecraft herself, of course, represents the small number of women who *were* well-educated—usually by fathers whose own excellent education led them to defy the trends of the day.

Another problem identified by feminist writers of the late eighteenth and nineteenth centuries was the lack of opportunity for women to support themselves if necessary in socially acceptable ways. The middle-class woman who didn't marry or found herself abandoned or widowed in financial straits often had to depend on the charity of better-off relatives, not always given graciously. In Britain almost her only option for self-support was to become a governess; and while such a position might be acceptable, it was often attended by a lack of respect from her employers and a social consciousness of loss of respectability. Also, her job might be made impossible by the lack of discipline in the home.

Even as late as 1907, women were still pointing out the need for entry into more professions than just teaching. M. Carey Thomas, a professor at Bryn Mawr (women's) College and its president from 1894-1922, protested that teaching should not be the only profession open to women, as not all women are fit for it: "They must be trained so as to find ready admission into the professions and into different kinds of business activity" (96) in order for their particular talents to be used and their creativity to be developed.

Earlier, in 1875, Susan B. Anthony had addressed the problem from a different perspective, suggesting that the destitution of many women had led to rampant prostitution that would be eradicated only through the availability of education and respectable employment. And she pointed out a cause for the increase in destitution among women that has been often overlooked: the removal from the home of much industry that once occupied women and allowed them to contribute to the family's well-being both through providing necessities and earning income.

"In the olden times, when [women] were occupied with useful and profitable work in the household, getting the meals and washing the dishes three times in every day of every year, doing the baking, the brewing, the washing and the ironing, the whitewashing, the butter and cheese and soap making, the mending and the making of clothes for the entire family, the carding, spinning, and weaving of the cloth—when everything to eat, to drink and to wear was manufactured in the home, almost no young women 'went out to work.' But now, when nearly all these handicrafts are turned over to men and to machinery, tens of thousands . . . of the women of both hemispheres are thrust into the world's outer market of work to earn their own subsistence. Society, ever slow to change its conditions, presents to these [women] but few and meager chances. Only the barest necessities, and oftentimes not even those, can be purchased with the proceeds of the most excessive and exhausting labor" (161).

Arnold Toynbee, writing in 1884, notes that the small farmer in England began to disappear with the improvement of technology and the buying up of land by the wealthier classes. He

notes as well that "the gradual destruction of domestic industries" affected their ability to stay on the land; through these and
other causes, families who had once supported themselves on the
land were forced to move to the cities to eke out a living in the
factories and sweatshops (38). Though he doesn't address the
direct effect on women, common sense suggests that Anthony
was correct. When it was no longer profitable to produce certain
items at home, money had to be made to buy them; when that
money could not be made from cottage industries and the husband's income was insufficient, as it often was, his wife and children were forced with him into factories and the deplorable
conditions of factory work—another problem addressed by feminists and other reformers of the nineteenth century.

Along with poor, even horrific factory conditions for women
and children who had to work in them, women faced other
problems that needed legal redress. Many feminists claimed that
women would never be equal to men until they were no longer
treated as men's property under the law, thus needing not only
opportunity for jobs but also legal rights that they were denied.
A marriage document signed by Lucy Stone (a prominent
American suffragist) and Henry Blackwell protested such legal
rights of a husband as "the custody of the wife's person," "the
exclusive control and guardianship of their children," "the sole
ownership of [the wife's] personal [estate], and use of her real
estate," and "the absolute right to the product of her industry"
(Kraditor, 149-150). In an ideal marriage, perhaps such rights
would be moot, but in a certain class of nineteenth-century society at least, where marriages were made for money and prestige
with little or no basis in mutual esteem, the laws effectively prevented a woman from any recourse if her person, her property,
or her children were abused.

Anthony, in her address on "Social Purity," pleads for "equal

power in the making, shaping and controlling of the circumstances of life" (162), specifically through the ballot. Suffrage,
of course, had originally been limited in both Great Britain and
the U.S. to property owners, and thus, by definition, to men
only. In the U.S. this qualification was abandoned as early as
1796 by Tennessee and 1826 by New York; in Great Britain,
property qualifications were mostly abandoned by 1867. To
Anthony, the vote was imperative because she believed that only
when women were equally represented in political life would
they be able to influence moral life. The painful sexual double
standard of the day—it is fine for men to patronize prostitution,
but any woman who is less than perfectly discreet is the dregs of
society—Anthony particularly deplored. Concerning all the relations between men and women, she says, "Neither in the making nor executing of the laws regulating these relations has
woman ever had the slightest voice. The statutes for marriage
and divorce, for adultery, breach of promise, seduction, rape,
bigamy, abortion, infanticide—all were made by men . . . with
no women's voices heard in our courts save as accused or witness, and in many cases the married woman is denied the poor
privilege of testifying as to her own guilt or innocence of the
crime charged against her" (165).

Harriot K. Hunt, who only after many struggles earned a
medical degree, sent to the Boston authorities each year with her
taxes a letter of protest. In it, she pointed out that women were
taxed without representation and were the only class of people
who could never obtain the right to vote. She also noted a particular instance in which women were harmed by this depriva-
tion, in that state-supported colleges and professional schools
were open only to men, although women's taxes supported them
and women would benefit from such higher education: It would
"save them from lives of frivolity and emptiness, [and] open the

way to many useful and lucrative pursuits, and so raise them above that degrading dependence, so fruitful a source of female misery" (230).

Ernestine Rose, in an 1851 speech to the Women's Rights Convention in Worcester, Massachusetts, deplored the many legal inequalities women faced, showing how they were considered to be property of, rather than companions to, their husbands. A particularly telling example is that of the judge who sentenced one man to six months imprisonment for stealing a pair of boots while giving another a mere reprimand for committing assault and battery against his wife. With particular eloquence, Rose pointed out the many ways in which men and women are alike and should thus be considered as equals before the law: "Like man, woman comes involuntarily into existence; like him, she possesses physical and mental and moral powers, on the proper cultivation of which depends her happiness; like him she is subject to all the vicissitudes of life; like him she has to pay the penalty for disobeying nature's laws, and far greater penalties has she to suffer from ignorance of her more complicated nature; like him she enjoys or suffers with her country. Yet she is not recognized as an equal!" (224).

These problems were real and needed resolution, but what was their source? A look at the prevailing views of woman and her place in society is enlightening. We have already noted that the newly wealthy middle class had begun imitating upper-class behavior and values, in particular the prestige associated with having sufficient means for a wife to be relieved of real work in the home through the keeping of servants and the buying of factory-made goods. And this value seems to have led to a particular view of women becoming prevalent among those wealthy enough to embrace it: Woman is "The Angel in the House," as Patmore calls her in his famous poem. Woman was "too good" to harm her sensibilities and sully her character by allowing her to have contact with the world. Instead, she was to stay by the hearth and turn her husband and children into good people by the quiet influence of her angelic nature. Some men even claimed that woman is morally and spiritually superior to man and mustn't endanger her purity by venturing away from the hearth into the rough-and-tumble world of men.

Writer and editor Orestes A. Brownson says woman is "endowed with patience, endurance, passive courage, quick sensibilities, a sympathetic nature, and great executive and administrative ability. She was born to be a queen in her own household, and to make home cheerful, bright and happy." As a helpmeet and mother, she is perfect. To her children she is fit to be "their nurse, their early instructress, their guardian, their life-long friend"; to her husband, "his companion, his comforter, his consoler in sorrow, his friend in trouble, his ministering angel in sickness" (193). Senator George G. Vest, in arguing against women's suffrage, says that woman is better than man, and that giving her the vote will "take her down from that pedestal where she is today, influencing as a mother the minds of her offspring, influencing by her gentle and kindly caresses the action of her husband toward the good and the pure." He says that woman's ascribed sphere of family, a sphere of "the heart," is best for her: "the realm of sentiment, the realm of love, the realm of the gentler and the holier and kindlier attributes that make the name of wife, mother, and sister next to that of God Himself" (196).

Woman, clergyman Jonathon F. Stearnes says, is in fact entrusted by God with the special custody of religion. If she enters the realm of the world through the vote or through professions outside the home, the nation will, "rejecting the civilities of life, and throwing off the restraints of morality and piety . . . become a fierce race of semi-barbarians, before whom neither order, nor

honor, nor chastity can stand" (50). "Grace, modesty, and loveliness are the charms which constitute [woman's] power,"
William and Mary College professor Thomas R. Dew assures us.
"By these, she creates the magic spell that subdues to her will the
more mighty physical powers by which she is surrounded." Her
power comes from being weak and dependent, and by "delight-
ing and fascinating" her husband, she can "make him an humble suppliant at her shrine" (46).

What paragons of virtue these men seem to make of women!
Perhaps it is not too difficult to understand why Virginia Woolf
writes of her battle to kill "the angel of the house" so that she
could write. Yet, often in the same breath with these high and
holy views of woman's morality, her spirituality, her ability to
influence men and children to that which is good and pure, men
tell us that she is too weak and irrational—and even immoral—
to dare show herself in public and take part in any social, vocational, or political concerns outside the family hearth.

Brownson, for example, immediately following his
encomium on the virtues of women, says, "We do not believe
women, unless we acknowledge individual exceptions, are fit to
have their own head [i.e., govern themselves]." Indeed, women
too readily seduce men from the proper path as, he claims, Eve
did to Adam, and it is solely through the influence of women
that any man would become a "hideous monster," which is how
he describes women who are ungoverned by men, who are "free
to follow [their] own fancies and vague longings, [their] own
ambition and natural love of power" (193). New York legisla-
tor Abraham L. Kellog, after also expressing lofty sentiments
about women, says, "A few of the excellent and worthy women
who are in this Convention demanding the right to vote, I con-
cede would do so [wisely]. There are thousands of bad women
who would also vote, at least, upon some questions, thus enforc-

ing upon millions of modest and retiring mothers responsibilities from which they shirk, and rightly so" (198).

Perhaps the backhanded compliments of Grover Cleveland best sum up the contradictions and patronizing airs that angered the small number of educated women of the day. Women's special qualities are "weaknesses" or "frailties" that give her "strength" in the home sphere, Cleveland says. She is "not gifted with the power of clear and logical thinking," but she does have "intuition," which shows her "abstract moral truths." She "deals mistakenly with practical problems" because of her "sympathy and sentiment" that "cloud her perception" of the issues. She is "unbusinesslike" because of her "trustfulness and charitableness." She is "stubborn" because "her beliefs take a strong hold on her." The crowning insult is: "If she is sometimes fitful and petulant it is but the prelude to bright smiles and sunny endearments" (199).

I would not want my children raised by the kind of woman Cleveland describes. In fact, he and many other men of the time insult women by suggesting that they are actually not capable of balancing their natural sensitivity and emotion with reason and clarity of thought. And I fail to understand how this "woman" who is the fountain of spirituality and morality is the same "woman" who is an evil seductress who will destroy the entire fabric of the nation if she gains so much as a vote. And these contradictions—extremes, both of which contain some truth but neither of which correctly identifies the nature of woman—are, I think, at the heart of the social and legal problems experienced by women that led to the eighteenth- and nineteenth-century feminist movement. To say that woman is either virtually perfect or the primary source of all sin—or both at the same time—can only lead to distortions of the laws and practices that govern her, such as those we have seen.

These early feminists were hardly either paragons of virtue or evil seductresses. They were intelligent and highly educated (some self-educated, some educated by their fathers, some through highly unusual and strongly resisted excursions into colleges) and cared deeply for issues other than their own. In fact, most of the earliest feminists in America were first passionate abolitionists and prohibitionists, often beginning to espouse women's rights because of the criticisms leveled against them for speaking publicly about those other issues. As members of the middle and upper classes, they understood that they held a privileged place in society and desired to see the lot of poor women improved not only through their individual or institutional efforts but through the passage of laws that would better protect them from unscrupulous men. Most were religiously devout, held marriage and motherhood in high esteem, and did not see men as "the enemy" to be hated and vanquished, but as fellow humans who needed to be persuaded to see the reasonableness of women's demands and help them come about. And their opinion seems to have been vindicated by the fact that the majority of reforms they desired had been at least started before women ever received the vote, and generally in a manner proposed by the feminists themselves.

Mary Wollstonecraft, for example, proposed a system of public education in which children would attend day schools, boys and girls together—not much different from what is common in both Britain and the U.S. today. Judith Sargent Murray proposed that girls, as well as boys, be taught such subjects as astronomy, geography, and natural philosophy so they would be able to think about matters of substance when they went about their daily tasks as wives and mothers and thus avoid the temptations of gossip and vanity. The first women's college opened its doors in London in 1848; by 1900 twelve colleges and universities offered degrees to women, and women could study at Oxford and Cambridge. In the U.S., the first women's college opened as early as 1821, and Oberlin became the first coed college in 1833, with the University of Iowa the first state college to admit women in 1855. At the turn of the century, M. Carey Thomas pled with colleges who were finally admitting women not to develop courses that would benefit them solely in the practical aspects of homemaking. These, she said, belonged in professional schools, and women should first receive a liberal education; precisely because most of them will marry and have children, they "cannot conceivably be given an education too broad, too high, too deep to fit them to become the educated mothers of the future race of men and women to be born of educated parents" (95). Today, of course, virtually all colleges admit women, offer them a liberal arts education, and hold out opportunities for graduate work as well; and in fact more women than men today attend college as undergraduates and in master's degree programs.

Primarily because of the new educational opportunities, occupational opportunities have also vastly increased for women. While teaching remains a common professional avenue for them, more and more are entering business ventures in various roles, and more are becoming health professionals and working in the sciences and industry as well as in the arts and the media. In both Britain and the U.S., women have been free to enter any profession they wish since World War I, and though entrance into some professions has been difficult, determined women have led the way. Job sharing, now becoming a reality in some workplaces, was even suggested by Antoinette Brown Blackwell in 1873, so that women with young children could have a respite from household chores while performing work that would use their particular talents and interests. Today home businesses—for a time illegal in many communities—offer even more opportunities for self-support or extra family income, especially with the advent of the Internet.

On the legal scene, reform laws in both the U.S. and Britain began addressing working conditions in the factories for women and children before the end of the nineteenth century, with restrictions on the number of hours employees could be required to work, restrictions on child labor, requirements for basic safety conditions, etc. In the U.S., the first women's unions were formed in 1868 and began lobbying successfully for laws to protect women workers; in 1872, female federal employees were guaranteed equal pay for equal work. In Britain, the Married Women's Property Acts, passed from 1870-1908, gave women the right to keep and control property upon marriage and after, as well as inheritance rights. The vote, which all the feminists considered so vitally important, was given to women in 1918 in Britain, and the Nineteenth Amendment was ratified in the U.S. in 1920.

The specific goals of the early feminists, then, have been largely met; laws exist for redress of particular instances of discrimination or abuse. Women are as free as they have ever been, freer than perhaps in any other era of history. The many rights we now take for granted were won by perseverance and dedicated action, often at a personal cost most of us would find hard to pay. For that, we can and should be thankful to those who came before us.

And yet modern feminists seem just as discontent as—and much angrier than—their predecessors. We will look at the reasons in the next chapter, but the seeds of modern radical feminism and the feminist movement in the church were sown in the assumptions and philosophies of the same women who brought about those much-needed reforms from which we benefit.

One of the early feminists' important assumptions was that women need economic independence from men. This must have seemed like simple logic to women like Wollstonecraft and Anthony who saw the effects of a legal system that treated women as property and as incapable of handling money or property themselves. When whatever property a woman owned automatically became her husband's upon marriage, when any wages she earned legally belonged to him, when she could not inherit property or handle monies left to her except through a male executor, when she had no recourse in law if the property that had been hers was wasted by her husband in profligacy, her economic dependence must have seemed a great evil.

Anthony said that as long as these conditions existed, women's position in society would never change. "Marriage," she claimed, "will never cease to be a wholly unequal partnership until the law recognizes the equal ownership in the joint earnings and possessions" (164). This was not a call for women to leave the home for careers, but a call to recognize the contributions of a woman to her marriage and to make her a true partner to her husband before the law. Also a problem was the dependence of single women on family members after a husband's death; because few opportunities existed for respectable employment, these women became charity cases instead of productive citizens. Economic independence for all women, then, came to represent freedom from the "enslavement" created by unjust laws.

Another important assumption made by the earlier feminists has to do with the equality of men and women. They saw men and women as equal in personhood, intelligence, and morality, but readily conceded that women were specially suited for domestic affairs while men, by virtue of physical strength and the absence of the natural biological responsibility for children, were better suited for protection and provision. All they wished for was the opportunity to prove their equality where there *should* be no differences, including in arenas outside the home itself. Murray reminds men of their ideal partnership with their wives: "You are by nature formed for our protectors; we pretend not to vie with you in bodily strength. . . . Shield us then, we beseech you, from external evils, and in return *we* will transact *your* domestick affairs. Yes, *yours*, for are you not equally interested in these matters with ourselves?" (37). Women had a sacred responsibility to husband and children but wished to fulfill it with dignity and wished for women without those responsibilities to live with dignity as well.

However, in their emphasis on equality, they rejected the idea of man's leadership in any arena of life, broadening the concept of economic independence to general independence. This stance was at least partly a response to the false teachings of the time that men were actually superior beings to women in their intellectual and moral capabilities. Clergyman Henry Grew proclaimed in a debate in Philadelphia with feminists that "it was clearly the will of God that man should be superior in power and authority to woman" ("Debate," 108). An 1852 editorial in the New York *Herald* claimed that woman is by her nature subject to man "just as the negro is and always will be, to the end of time, inferior to the white race, and, therefore, doomed to subjection" ("The Woman's Rights," 190). In reaction to these kinds of ideas, a resolution by the women at the Second Worcester Convention in 1851 reads: "We deny the right of any portion of the species to decide for another portion, or of any individual to decide for another individual what is and what is not their 'proper sphere'" ("Resolutions," 221). Angelina Emily Grimke likened women to slaves also, because both classes of people were being judged by something inherent in their biological nature that couldn't be changed and had nothing to do with their personhood. "Human beings have *rights* because they are *moral* beings," she explains; therefore, "the *mere circumstance of sex* does not give to men higher rights and responsibilities, than to women" (62).

These assumptions about independence and equality rose from philosophies that, even for the devout, placed human reason—based on experience and scientific discovery—above the revelation of Scripture. Wollstonecraft, who was something of a freethinker but believed deeply in a God who is concerned with His creation both now and for eternity, typifies the philosophy of many of the devout feminists in her combination of Scripture and reason. Early on in *Vindication*, she asks the question: "In what does man's pre-eminence over the brute creation consist?" and answers it: "The answer is as clear as that a half is less than the whole; in Reason" (12). Yet as frequently as she appeals to reason (virtue is the effect of an educated reason, she says), she appeals to the divine: God is the source of reason, and "I build my belief on the perfection of God" (15). She appeals to the fact of God's creation of mankind to support her plea for women to be educated properly; if woman has a soul and is intended to live eternally, surely she should be developing her intellect and her moral sense in this world.

Others more explicitly placed reason above Scripture, though still clinging to the fundamental ideas of Christianity. Some simply said that while the Bible had much of value in it, it could not be relied on above reason. "I do not want to dwell too much upon Scripture authority," said Lucretia Mott in the debate with Grew. "We too often bind ourselves by authorities rather than truth" ("Debate," 111). Others developed elaborate arguments to show that Scripture could be interpreted to mean that men and women were absolute equals, and no differences existed in the activities each could do, even in the church. These arguments are for the most part identical to those posed today by feminists in the church, which we will look at in Chapter 4.

Others—though these were not many—threw out Scripture altogether for reliance on man's reason or scientific ideas of the time. William Lloyd Garrison, in the Philadelphia debate, appealed to "nature" and the Declaration of Independence for proof of women's equality to men: "The human mind is greater than any book," he said of Grew's appeal to the Bible. "We must look at things rationally" ("Debate," 112). Some feminists similarly relied on science, as that discipline was gaining force in society through the evolutionary ideas gaining popularity through Darwin's *The Origin of Species*. Matilda Joslyn Gage uses Darwinian philosophy to claim that "woman possesses in a higher degree than man that adaptation to the conditions surrounding her which is everywhere accepted as evidence of superior vitality and higher physical rank in society" (140), and Elizabeth Cady Stanton appeals to science for proof that humankind began as matriarchal and that man's eventual physical domination has since caused all the evils of society.

The "science" these feminists relied on has been proven false or open to legitimate question; their reliance on "reason" is often as much a reliance on experience as logic. In both cases, of course, their rejection of Scripture as the final authority leaves them without a standard by which to judge their ideas and assumptions. In the next chapter we will see the effect of such philosophies in the wholly secular feminist movement that began after World War II and, in the chapter following, the effect on feminism in the church.

CHAPTER THREE

Twentieth-Century Radicalism

ᕯ

We in the church must be concerned with two kinds of feminism today: the radical secular feminism that is creating havoc in our culture, and a less vitriolic feminism that many say is doing the same within the church. As we shall see, secular feminism today results from shifts in circumstances and worldview, though it shares many of the assumptions of earlier feminism. The feminism promoted within the church is the logical result of earlier feminism stripped of its altruistic element. Secular feminism is the subject of this chapter, feminism in the church of the next.

After most of the clearly defined goals of the early feminists were met—legal, educational, and vocational rights along with the right to vote—the women's movement died out as a national entity. Some women were still working for further specific changes or to rectify individual instances of discrimination, but most women simply took advantage of their new rights and raised their daughters in a culture that took these rights for granted. My girlfriends and I expected to attend college, knew we could have a career in any field we wished to pursue, looked forward to the first election after we turned eighteen, and never once considered ourselves disadvantaged or discriminated against. So when a new feminist movement began in the mid-sixties and seventies, we didn't understand. What more could these women want anyway?

Betty Friedan would have considered us naive, I suppose, and in some ways we were. But when I read *The Feminine Mystique*, I was baffled. The book purported to describe my mother's generation; yet no woman I knew fit the description. More knowledgeable now, I understand that Friedan has accurately captured the misery and malaise of a certain segment of the middle-class population of the mid-sixties. Certainly the book resonated with many suburban women, touching off a revolution that has transformed American culture perhaps more than any other single work, with the possible exception of *Uncle Tom's Cabin*.

Friedan claimed that women needed to gain back the rights they had somehow, after World War II, lost—not in law but in practice. To make her point, she chronicled the "quiet desperation" of suburban wives and mothers of the early sixties. She claimed to have found full-time housewives all over the country who were miserable and frustrated, discontent with their lives but not knowing why or what to do about it, and feeling guilty for their discontent. "I just don't feel alive," women told her. "My days are all busy, and dull too." "By noon I'm ready for a padded cell." "You wake up one morning and there's nothing to look forward to." She painted this "problem that has no name" in the bleakest of colors: "*Each* suburban wife struggled with it alone. As she made the beds, shopped for groceries, matched slipcover material, ate peanut butter sandwiches with her children, chauffeured Cub Scouts and Brownies, lay beside her husband at night—she was afraid to ask even of herself the silent question—'Is this all?'" (15, emphasis mine).

Why did so many women seem so unhappy? Friedan wondered. As she explored the "problem that has no name," she began to see patterns in these women's lives that offered a possible cause: They lived solely through their husbands and children, had no interests of their own, and filled all of their time with the relatively easy tasks of housekeeping. She seemed appalled to find that some women were refusing to buy dishwashers or had begun making their own bread and sewing their own clothes, even though there was no economic need for them to do so, "just to fill the time." Her analysis of the suburban housewife's problem? "The more your intelligence exceeds your job requirements, the greater your boredom" (251).

In other words, housewives weren't using their talents and education and as a result were drowning in boredom and self-pity. Basic housekeeping tasks in the twentieth century don't require an inordinate amount of skill and creativity, laborsaving devices abound, and these women weren't finding the volunteer work available in their communities particularly challenging either. But why, with the legal opportunity and financial means to do anything they wished, did they not pursue activities that would use their abilities more fully, either in jobs outside the home or in creative work (such as writing or painting) from within the home? The colleges were open to them, but if they took classes it was only to dabble in a variety of nonacademically demanding subjects. If volunteer work led to the offer of administrative positions that might have used more talent, women tended to turn down the offers. Because women who tried to work from home didn't discipline themselves to excel, their work remained amateurish and of little value.

Friedan decided that the cause of these problems was the development of a new "feminine mystique." Remember the "angel in the house" image that early feminists protested against? For some reason, Friedan believed, that image had reared its fantastic head again, and women had come to believe it, had come to believe that they should want nothing more than to be wives and mothers who lived solely for the family and had no interests outside it. She suggested possible sources of the image—the war had left everyone with a desire for cozy home life, women were less welcome in the workplace now that the soldiers had returned needing jobs to support families, advertisers saw the potential in marketing home products to a large number of women with the means to be reliable consumers. Whatever the cause, there it was. And pampered husbands resented it if wives wanted a life outside the home; employers couldn't understand why a woman would want to work, discriminating against them in hiring and wages because of the assumption that they would leave for marriage or childbearing; and women themselves felt guilty if life at home wasn't "enough" to satisfy their needs.

Friedan's solution? Women needed to have a commitment to something outside the home, a purpose larger than housekeeping that would give meaning to their lives: careers. She went so far as to say, "I am convinced that there is something in the housewife state itself that is dangerous" (305). The only place women could use their intelligence and talent in a way that had value and would be fulfilling was in a career outside the home. She conceded that before modern technology a home had so much varied and creative work that a woman truly contributed to the economic welfare of the home and could find a sense of self there; but this is no longer possible in the modern world, she was convinced. In fact, motherhood and homemaking should be "fitted into" a woman's life around her much more important career. She finally claimed that women can "find identity only in work that is of real value to society—work for which, usually, our society pays" (346).

And the women she spoke with who either had careers or were pursuing definite action to move into careers (college work, training) certainly sounded more sure of themselves and happier. They spoke of better marriages and happier children as well as a personal sense of well-being and accomplishment. Friedan puts it, "They knew that it did not come from the work alone, but from the whole—their marriage, homes, children, work, their changing, growing links with the community. They were once again human beings, not 'just housewives'" (356).

Friedan is not anti-male. She believes that love ought to be part of a woman's life: "The assumption of your own identity, equality, and even political power does not mean you stop needing to love, and be loved by, a man, or that you stop caring for your kids. I would have lost my own feeling for the women's movement if I had not been able, finally, to admit tenderness" (395). And, in fact, she has much of value to say. She is right that living exclusively for one's family is not healthy—living for them in the sense that a woman has no other purpose in life save to live *through* them, find all her meaning in them. Such a woman indulges her children so that they grow up believing the world owes them the same care as she has given them; such a woman finally frustrates and alienates her children by her hovering and hand-holding, and her husband by her obsessive need for his constant attention and companionship and approval.

Friedan notes that Dr. A. H. Maslow, in his studies of people who realize their potential ("self-actualizers"), says that they have "some mission in life, some task to fulfill, some problem outside themselves which enlists much of their energies. . . . In general these tasks are nonpersonal or unselfish, concerned rather with the good of mankind in general, or of a nation in general" (quoted on 322). And she is right when she says that "the chains that bind [woman] in her trap are chains in her own mind and spirit. They are chains made up of mistaken ideas and misinterpreted facts, of incomplete truths and unreal choices" (31).

Sadly, however, Friedan herself has given us "incomplete truths" based on "mistaken ideas and misinterpreted facts." Yes, many of the women she spoke with were miserable because they had no purpose other than to live for and through their families. And it appeared that when women chose to pursue careers, their misery disappeared and the entire family benefited. However, in her insistence that a paid career outside the home for the purpose of self-fulfillment is imperative for a woman's happiness, Friedan has missed the point, a point made even in the Maslow quotation she cites. Thousands of women now pursue careers in the search for self-fulfillment, but self-fulfillment never comes when we seek it; it comes only in seeking the fulfillment of others. Only by losing self can we find self. So if we are doing anything—marrying, mothering, working for pay, volunteering—for the purpose of finding ourselves, *we will remain unfulfilled.* Only if the "larger purpose" we find takes us out of ourselves can we discover the sense of self-worth and satisfaction that God intended us to enjoy in service to Him and our neighbor.

This is why *The Feminine Mystique* seemed so alien to me. My mother and her friends, and many women I know today, are completely and genuinely content to be full-time homemakers. This is because they understand the value of the job. Molding children into productive, moral citizens is no easy task, but it is fulfilling. These mothers don't indulge their children, doing everything for them and protecting them from adversity and pain. They do a much more difficult job—they train their children to become responsible, caring adults. Many of these same women bake their own bread and sew their own clothes too, not because they need more tasks to fill their time, but because it is good stewardship of money and health, as well as giving their children life-skill training in those areas.

What drives these women and makes them happy is a purpose outside themselves. They know they are fulfilling the vocation God gave them as women, and they understand the value of mothers in their children's lives and of wives in their husbands' lives. Their family is a gift and a ministry, and even housework—irksome in its repetitiveness as any job certainly can be—affords an opportunity to serve others and train their children in developing responsibility and a servant attitude. They are servants who find as they serve their families that they become more and more the unique individuals God created them to be. And these same women almost always take their servant hearts outside the home into church and community activities and maybe even into the business or political arena, not to "fulfill themselves" but because they see needs that they know God has called them to meet.

In fact, this is also a primary difference from the feminists present at the new movement's inception. In both cases, the women who are part of feminism are middle- and upper-class women of privilege. The early feminists like Stanton and Anthony explicitly recognized this and did not claim that they themselves had particularly suffered from oppression. Instead, they looked at those who were truly victimized—the poor—and sought legal changes that would end their exploitation by unscrupulous men who used unfair laws to their own advantage. But the feminists of the sixties and following have had one primary purpose that underlies all their actions: the drive for personal fulfillment and contentment. They are *themselves* the oppressed whose cause they champion, and while they might lobby for, say, better Social Security benefits for older women, their energy is primarily expended on causes that benefit themselves, such as "reproductive rights" (i.e., government-funded abortion and abortion and birth control for minors without parental consent or notification), lesbian rights, affirmative action, and silencing the right-wing conservatives (especially Christians) who disagree with their agenda.

Even Friedan's insistence on the need for economic independence for women is based on a different motivation from the early feminists. Anthony and others saw that laws that gave women no economic rights whatsoever allowed unscrupulous men to take advantage of their wives. She was not, however, claiming that all women needed to work in jobs outside the home, for any reason. Rather, she wished to see economic justice so that if a man divorced or abandoned his wife, she would have a share in the income her work at home had helped him gain and thus could still survive financially rather than facing destitution. Listen, on the other hand, to Friedan on economic independence: "Equality and human dignity are not possible for women if they are not able to earn. . . . Only economic independence can free a woman to marry for love, not for status or financial support, or to leave a loveless, intolerable, humiliating marriage, or to eat, dress, rest, and move if she plans not to marry" (385).

But women *had* the right to work in virtually any job they might choose at the time Friedan wrote this. No woman had to marry to gain financial security. No single woman was being kept from earning her way. Perhaps all conditions everywhere were not ideal, but opportunities still abounded. Yet these are not the real reasons Friedan is concerned with economic independence; the first sentence of the quote tells us the real reason. Friedan has chosen to see human equality and value in economic terms: It is not *possible*, she says, to have dignity without earning a wage. This is why she so devastatingly demeans the role of the full-time housewife—such a woman has no "dignity"; as other feminists would say, more harshly, she is a leech on her husband and society.

Though Friedan implies that a woman might need to devote a larger amount of time to her children at least until they are in school, keeping herself involved in her interests through part-time or volunteer work or continuing education rather than a full-time job, the tone of the entire book suggests that mothering is merely an interruption to the real satisfactions of career, and housework is invariably dull and degrading, unnecessary and unimportant. For women who see no purpose in it, of course this is true; if a woman's larger purpose in life is to fulfill herself through the use of her talents in a job that pays her and gives her prestige, then of course housework and mothering seem onerous and unfulfilling tasks. Friedan even goes so far as to suggest, in the words of a study she cites, that women who don't have "ambition," who don't want recognition or money for the work they do in the church or community, must be "fooling themselves" (quoted on 355). They are pretending not to care about something they really must want. Again, we see Friedan's emphasis on an economic evaluation of personal worth: The amount you earn—and the prestige of the job you hold—determine your worthiness as a human being.

But who is going to do that dull and degrading housework while Mom fulfills herself? Who is going to take care of her children as they learn to walk and talk and become social and moral beings? *Other women.* Poorer women who can't afford the training necessary for the fulfilling jobs or—do the feminists perhaps think—who lack the intelligence or drive to pursue them? Aren't women exploiting other women when they pay them low wages to do what they themselves find demeaning or unfulfilling? Or is it only men who can exploit women? Sadly, the radical feminists answer that last question with a resounding yes. In fact, they would say that *all* men exploit *all* women—a concept that explains their radical attempts to restructure the society for the sake of "fairness" to women.

That question my friends and I asked back in the sixties and seventies has a quite different answer than it would have had at the turn of the century. What *do* these women want? The early feminists had gained legal equality for them; yet still they feel oppressed, believing men are holding them back despite legal freedom. So what they really want is *social* equality; they want men to change their *attitudes* toward women. Thus they began seeking ways to restructure the society to make it more comfortable for women—or at least for themselves. Friedan, in her 1973 epilogue to *Mystique*, makes this quite clear: "The changes necessary to bring about that equality were, and still are, very revolutionary indeed. They involve a sex-role revolution for men and women which will restructure all our institutions: child-rearing, education, marriage, the family, the architecture of the home, the practice of medicine, work, politics, the economy, religion, psychological theory, human sexuality, morality, and the very evolution of the race" (384).

An ambitious project indeed. And one that has been taken most seriously by the radical feminists who evolved from the new feminism of Friedan and her generation. The National Organization for Women was spawned from the response to *Mystique* and has had tremendous influence in the forming of attitudes and public policy. "You can have it all," Friedan said to the American woman, and NOW has pledged to make sure no woman is held back from anything she wants.

Unless, of course, what she wants is antithetical to the agenda of NOW.

Take a look around the NOW web site (www.now.org).

You'll find plenty about affirmative action and violence against women, lesbian and abortion rights, sexual harassment and the horrors of the oppressive "religious right"—but nothing that would suggest that marriage and motherhood are of value to most women. Although they claim to support any woman's right to work as a homemaker, the only action they appear to have actually taken to benefit homemakers is the popularizing of the slogan "every mother is a working mother" and the coining of the phrase "women who work outside the home." The goals listed for helping homemakers are to gain recognition for the economic value of their contributions to family and society and "legislation and programs reflecting the reality of marriage as an equal economic partnership." Yet looking at actions actually taken, none are of direct or even indirect benefit to the full-time homemaker. In fact, many of the policy demands, such as government-funded day care, will ultimately force more unwilling women into the workplace for the economic survival of their families. The one specific policy goal they claim to want for homemakers—Social Security benefits—would actually raise their husbands' taxes and make it harder for them to stay at home. The Industrial Revolution forced women to work for basic necessities; the feminist revolution may force them to work to pay taxes.

NOW has moved increasingly away from any mainstream women's concerns and values as its members become increasingly out of touch with the lives of ordinary women. A *World Magazine* report on the 1999 NOW National Conference in Beverly Hills, California, describes the events: workshops that focus on airing complaints of all the ways the feminists have been lately offended (such as the woman upset over a magazine cover that featured a male athlete instead of a female); a speech denouncing capitalism by one of NOW's cofounders (which drew a standing ovation in spite of the plush locale of the conference); a lesbian poet who "entertained" the crowd with two "vile, divisive, male-hating, profane creations she called poems"; plenty of booths for all the various factions of the organization (many of whom are arguing among themselves about what NOW should and shouldn't promote); plenty of informational material on lesbianism; and a "spiritual moment" that involved the use of a tom-tom, a rattle, and a rain-stick while the leader (an "ecumenical lesbian reverend") told the audience to "go within you and beyond you, to that which is spirit, which is sacred, which is divine in the way you understand it" (15).

Christina Hoff Sommers, W. H. Brady Fellow at the American Enterprise Institute in Washington, D. C., writes of today's radical feminists: "Our system cannot handle much more pressure from these muddled but determined women with their multistage theories and their metaphors about windows, mirrors, and voices, their workshops, and above all their constant alarms about the state of male-female relations in American society" (*Feminism*, 179). She is referring to those she calls "gender feminists"—women who believe that our society is a "patriarchy . . . in which the dominant gender works to keep women cowering and submissive," who feel driven to prove that "the oppression of women . . . is a structural feature of our society" (*Feminism*, 16). In her compelling exposé of this movement, *Who Stole Feminism?: How Women Have Betrayed Women*, Sommers shows us the motivations of the gender feminists, the distortions and inaccuracies of their research, and the harm they cause by diverting energy and funds from genuine needs in their fanatical zeal for a cause more deeply rooted in emotionalism and ideology than in facts and true compassion.

On the University of Maryland campus in 1993, students in a women's studies class distributed fliers and posters titled

"Notice: These Men Are Potential Rapists," followed by a list of dozens of men's names taken randomly from the student phone directory. At Vassar, when several students were falsely accused of date rape, the assistant dean of women students seemed unperturbed at the false accusations, claiming that it was a good experience to force the men to think about their attitudes toward women. These kinds of assumptions about men characterize gender feminism and result from the angry resentment that is its hallmark and the goal of "consciousness-raising" groups led by gender feminists. Sommers discusses how they use resentment to place men and women in polarized camps: If a woman has ever been badly treated by a man in any way, or knows another woman who has, she can be brought to apply her resentment of that act and person to all actions by all men. Feminist author Marilyn French claims that men—*all* men— hold women in subjection because all women "know" that men *can* be violent toward them. Therefore, men can merely be unfair or disrespectful to women and expect them to submit to it out of fear of violence. This is the conscious "system" she claims men use to enforce gender inequity. She claims as well that "the vast majority of men in the world" are disrespectful of and/or violent toward women (quoted in Sommers, *Feminism*, 43). And the gender feminists are experts at drawing women into this mind-set, using even their college classrooms as recruitment zones for their ideology.

Men, to the gender feminists, are the enemy. So these feminists have created an atmosphere of suspicion and distrust everywhere, pouncing on any possible word or action that could be construed as "sexist." At the Boston *Globe*, a senior editor was reprimanded and fined (the fine was later rescinded) for using a vulgar expression in a private conversation with a male colleague that one of the women on the staff happened to overhear.

The *Globe* feminists resent the noon basketball game, which is mostly made up of men, and the use of sports metaphors in news stories, reading into both evidence of men's attitudes of superiority, "old-boy" cliquishness, and violence. Sexual harassment policies are being devised for grade-schoolers and little girls taught to see all teasing from boys as sexual in nature because, according to "sex equity specialist" Sue Sattel, "serial killers tell interviewers they started sexually harassing at age 10, and got away with it" (quoted in Sommers, *Feminism*, 46).

Although these gender feminists don't represent even the majority of feminists, much less the majority of women, they are the ones whose ideology is driving legislative and academic decisions in our culture. If their ideology were based on sound research, those decisions would be improving the lot of American girls and women. Instead, while actually losing some of the gains made by the early feminists, they are causing real problems to be ignored or trivialized because of a wrong focus and are creating new problems altogether.

Because the gender feminists see the world as "us vs. them," in black and white terms, they are constantly on the alert for "oppressive" or "harassing" situations such as the one described above at the Boston *Globe*. In another workplace, a young man was forced to remove from his desk a picture of his wife in a bikini because it created a "hostile work environment" (Sommers, *Feminism*, 271). These are common events nowadays, and one effect of this oversensitivity is to reinstate the stereotypes the earlier feminists fought, such as women being too "fragile" to handle the "rough-and-tumble" world outside the home. Now instead of fainting at men's crudity, women seek legislation to protect their delicate sensibilities and share their "horror" stories with one another at conferences and in consciousness-raising groups to help others become as sensitive and resentful as they are. The emotionalism that Sommers describes as pervasive at gender feminist conferences (of which she has attended dozens) reinforces the stereotype that women, because they are emotional, cannot be rational. And in fact many of the gender feminists explicitly eschew what they call "vertical thinking" (logic, rationality, clear analysis), preferring emotional responses to observations about the world. Even excellence and achievement are seen as male constructs that shouldn't be used to pressure women into behaving like men instead of like women.

Sommers gives numerous examples of issues about which policy is being made based on invalid research promoted by the gender feminists. Domestic violence, for example, is a problem that needs to be addressed, but the facts about it have been distorted and concealed by the feminists themselves and by the media who promote their agenda. Estimates of violent domestic attacks on women range from two to six million per year, with one source claiming that 50 percent of married women suffer abuse, more than one-third of them repeatedly. However, in one of the most reputable studies done on the issue, Richard J. Gelles and Murray A. Strauss found that although women are more likely to be severely injured by domestic violence, women are also perpetrators of domestic violence just as often as men. And their estimate for the number of women severely abused in the course of a year? One hundred thousand. That's a hundred thousand too many, granted, but it's also 1,900,000 lower than the nearest estimation used to drive policy.

Why the discrepancy? One way of coming up with a figure is to take the results of studies done in high-risk areas—inner-city hospitals, for example—and project those statistics to all men and women. Another way, Sommers explains in detail, is "creative interpretation" of the results of valid studies such as the one done by Gelles and Strauss. This involves broadening the scope of "abuse" to include a partner stomping out of a room or swearing, events that occur frequently, and ignoring the fact that almost no women answer yes to questions involving severe physical abuse such as being beaten or choked. So the study results as publicized "show" that a large number of women are being "abused," which the reader generally assumes to mean violent and repeated battery since it is not defined—and the gender feminists get another government-funded women's shelter.

But will such shelters even be placed where the few truly abused women actually need them? Possibly not, if the placement of rape crisis centers is any indication. As with domestic violence, widely varying numbers of rapes are reported by various sources. And as with domestic violence, Sommers shows how the huge "scare" numbers are based on faulty or at least questionable research methods. The "one in four" number that is used by the gender feminists is almost certainly far too large; one in twenty or even as low as one in fifty is much more likely. Of course, this is still too many, but again, the real figures are too low to create the fear and resentment that the gender feminists specialize in—and too low to get more government money for rape crisis centers.

But these centers are being opened in the least-needed places: college campuses. Although the exact number of rapes that occur is hard to identify, since it is certainly an underreported crime, still it is a fact that poor neighborhoods are much more likely to have high occurrences of rape, and that college women are far less likely to experience rape than the general population of young women their age. Yet the feminists demand—and get—expensive centers with funding for lights and emergency telephones and awareness meetings and counseling for college campuses where often not a single rape is reported in the course of a year. Why? According to Sommers, "The fact that college women continue to get a disproportionate and ever-growing share of the very scarce public resources allocated for rape prevention and for aid to rape victims underscores how disproportionately powerful and *self-preoccupied* the campus feminists are despite all their vaunted concern for 'women' writ large" (*Feminism*, 221).

In education, similarly flawed—or improperly analyzed—studies have "shown" that girls suffer a severe drop in self-esteem after adolescence, which the gender feminists attribute to the patriarchal biases of the school system. They claim that boys receive more positive attention in the classroom than girls, and that girls are "silenced" and made to feel incapable of doing well. However, reputable studies find that in fact, if boys receive more attention it is because they need more discipline, and girls are doing better in school at every age, in every subject (having recently caught up in math and science), and by every measure such as attendance, overall grades, attitude, and plans for continuing education.

The poor research in each of these areas (and many others) has led to poor policy decisions, sometimes denying the existence of real problems that need to be addressed or even creating entirely new problems, but at best focusing resources in areas of lesser need. For instance, it has been shown that the large majority of men who abuse women are criminals with a history of violent crime against women *and men*. But because this does not fit well with the gender feminist theory that all men are violent, that fact is suppressed, and the public is made to believe that otherwise normal men commonly abuse women. Also, the Gelles and Strauss study shows that as many women as men are perpetrators of domestic violence. Yet where are the resources to help battered men? Where are the resources to help violent women learn to control their anger? They are nonexistent because the gender feminists refuse to admit that the problem exists; and, because of the kinds of power they have, the facts are buried from both the general public and the policy-makers.

Rape crisis centers, as we noted above, are being funded on college campuses where very few rapes occur; but the centers located in high-risk, poverty-stricken areas often cannot afford even to have counselors available at the time a crime occurs. So the feminists sit unproductively in their comfortable campus enclaves waiting for the crises that rarely occur while caring people struggle to find volunteers to help women in the less pleasant areas where crime is actually happening. And men are wrongly vilified, too, by the distorted figures trotted out again and again by the gender feminists. If indeed one in four women is a victim of rape, then perhaps "all" men are violent; but the facts belie that kind of generalization. The sensitivity training and date rape seminars are a waste of money that could be used to help women who are truly victims, rather than to engender needless fear and suspicion.

In education, the situation created by the gender feminists may be the worst. Their demands and influence have led to all kinds of senseless and perhaps harmful policies—guidelines for textbooks, for example. History guidelines require that women be treated "equally" with men; yet women have never had the same impact on history as men. So the books give more space to Betsy Ross (who may not have made that first flag after all) than Paul Revere, or Maria Mitchell (a nineteenth-century astronomer who discovered a comet) than to Albert Einstein. All of this leaves students with an inadequate and distorted view of history. In younger grades, pictures in the textbooks have become "gender-correct": Women are shown as firefighters and doctors, CEOs and engineers. Pictures of women as homemakers and mothers are apparently forbidden altogether. There is no way of knowing, of course, how such distortions of reality will affect children in the long run; there is concern that healthy gender formation may be at risk if children are given androgynous ideas about men and women (Levin, 96).

And the gender feminists' rejection of so-called "male vertical thinking" (logic and analysis) is helping destroy the math and science curricula as well. Feminist educator Peggy McIntosh, in a teacher-training seminar, discussed a young girl's difficulty with adding a column of numbers. The problem, as she saw it, "was that the worksheet required her to think vertically, thereby undermining her self-esteem and causing her to become discouraged." Her solution? Without suggesting any specific technique, she told the teachers "to find ways to 'put . . . [students] off the right-wrong axis, the win-lose axis'" (Sommers, *Feminism*, 174). Perhaps McIntosh believes that making the child "feel good about herself" whether or not she can add columns of numbers will suffice. However, we do know that, however good American children might feel about themselves and their abilities, they are consistently and substantially outscored by foreign children on math and science tests (National Center for Educational Statistics)—a problem area overlooked and thus not being solved because of the emphasis on "gender equity" that tries to make all students (including boys) into "feminine lateral thinkers" at the expense of precisely the skills that would bring up math proficiency. (Lateral thinking, according to McIntosh, is more "relational" and "inclusive"; the aim of a lateral thinker is "not to win, but to be in a decent relationship with the invisible elements of the universe" [quoted in Sommers, *Feminism*, 67]).

Now, thanks to the gender feminists, we also have the national Gender Equity Act to ensure that girls are not shortchanged in schools. This act set up a gender equity office in Washington, with a director to "promote, coordinate, and evaluate gender equity policies"—including millions of dollars' worth of local and state grants for research about the bias against girls in schools, teacher and community training, evaluation, resources, etc. Unfortunately, all of this money is being spent on a problem that in reality is nonexistent—unless we look at the significantly poorer performance of boys in school and define them as the ones being treated with discrimination. Sommers has done precisely this in her recent book, *The War Against Boys: How Misguided Feminism Is Harming Our Young Men.* She debunks all the so-called "evidence" of a "gender gap" in schools that favors boys and shows instead that it is young men who are losing out on education, often directly as a result of the policies demanded by gender feminists in the name of "equity."

Boys, now behind in every academic area, with greater risk of dropping out and not continuing past high school, are consistently ignored when it comes to talk of programs to help our students. Instead, as Sommers puts it, "As the plight of boys grows, with no relief in sight, programs for girls multiply" (*War*, 39). In New York in 1996, an all-girls school was opened in East Harlem. It was phenomenally successful, and Chancellor of Schools Rudy Crew was urged to open a similar school for boys. Crew refused because he "regarded the girls' school as reparatory for past educational practices that neglected girls"; he wished to "make a statement" about girls' education (*War*, 39). There are, however, many more African-American women in higher education than African-American men, and they succeed at much higher rates than the men who do attend college. Yet educators persist in refusing equal opportunity for the young men to develop the skills and attitudes necessary for their success.

That story is only one of many Sommers tells. She says those who promote "gender equity" in the schools "have a great deal of power . . . but they are far too reckless with the truth, far too removed from the precincts of common sense, and far too negative about boys to be properly playing any role in the education of our children. Yet their influence is growing" (*War*, 51). School districts are now forced to implement programs that favor girls and are often forced to back off from programs that would help boys because of a plethora of complex federal laws about gender equity. Literally millions of dollars are being poured into programs and policies that not only harm boys academically but even attack their nature as boys. Sommers describes one classroom where only pictures of women are on the walls, boys are forced to take on female roles in class presentations, discussions persistently revolve around how men are violent and desire only to oppress women, and the class project is the making of a quilt celebrating women. This, by the way, is a sixth-grade class, and even the girls, while they like the teacher, worry that the boys are being shortchanged. The girls who mention this concern, however, are merely considered to have low self-esteem because they have already learned from the culture that they are less worthy than boys.

How has such a small group of women managed to wield so much power? Sommers explains in *Who Stole Feminism?* that their power to influence has not come so much in the legislatures, where women, however radically feminist, are still substantially outnumbered, but rather by their gaining administrative power in the colleges and universities, as well as in the professional organizations of the academy. From these positions they are able to make or strongly influence budget decisions, personnel decisions, program decisions, etc. Many universities now ask questions in the interview process that evaluate a prospect's attitudes toward women and women's issues, and if the prospect gives the "wrong" answers, he or she will not be hired. Faculty without tenure are in grave danger of losing their positions if they do not support the gender feminists and their agenda; even faculty with tenure rarely cross them because of the very real possibility of lawsuits and forced resignation. Sommers believes that many faculty and college administrators do not understand the difference between gender feminists and feminists who advocate rational changes; they give in to gender feminist proposals in order to be "sensitive" to women. Others simply don't wish to fight the battle, hoping the movement will turn out to be a fad that will die of its own accord.

Many of the studies used (misused) by the gender feminists have originated in such prestigious academic organizations as the American Association of University Women (AAUW), which are expected by the media and legislators to provide high-quality, professional research projects and results. They do not, apparently, realize that these organizations have become more and more radically feminist-oriented over the past couple of decades and so have accepted without question studies shown to be massively flawed or results deliberately skewed to distort the truth. (Of course, many media women are gender feminists themselves, with tremendous influence in that industry as well.) The gender feminists have succeeded in creating a climate of fear and repression throughout the academy, in convincing the media that they represent all women and truthfully portray the problems of women, and in pushing through legislation that, if not directly harmful, is useless and wasteful.

And yet the gender feminists are more discontent than ever, in spite of all they have accomplished in trying to bring about their gender-neutral society. We have more laws, but people don't seem willing to change their whole thinking about all of life, even when forced to behave in certain ways in places that can be regulated, such as the office or classroom. True, there is sometimes real sexual harassment that needs to be addressed, or real wage or other discrimination. But laws exist already to address these. When women claim there are no differences between the sexes that should lead to differences in career options, when they demand quotas that are unrealistic given the numbers of women qualified or even wanting to follow certain careers, when they claim that women who fail to fulfill their professional responsibilities are victims of discrimination if reprimanded or fired, when they are willing to skew research data or make up false statistics, when they demand that people who disagree with them be silenced, then they display, it seems to me, a dissatisfaction that has less to do with external discrimination than with internal unrest.

This is the result of the modern feminists' focus on self-fulfillment, which is in turn a result of cultural shifts during the mid-twentieth century that supplied a fertile bed for their growth, starting with Friedan and quickly beginning to overrun the whole garden. More distance may be needed to analyze the exact changes and understand the reasons for them; however, some key changes surely include the surge of prosperity and materialism that followed the war, the emphasis on individualism in an increasingly relativistic climate, and an optimistic faith in the goodness of human nature.

The new prosperity allowed many more women to stay at home and to own the latest technologies that made housework easier, thus giving them more time on their hands and less with which to fill it. Friedan tells of her visit to an ad agency where she saw thousands of documents on how to sell material goods to women, slanting ads to appeal to their needs to feel creative and useful and modern while remaining ensconced in the home.

More leisure time led to a larger market for entertainment, and the ability to provide well for one's family led many to believe that God was superfluous, creating greater self-reliance and self-centeredness.

The U.S. has always been a nation of individualists, but at the beginning respect for the individual was tempered by an understanding of the sin nature and the need for restraints on all people, individuals as well as groups, so that power of any kind was not abused. As Dr. James Hitchcock of St. Louis University, in his article "What Went Wrong with the Fifties?" puts it, "Truly sensitive consciences are aware of precisely the ways in which they need external restraint, and hence always seek to embody morality in institutional forms" (16). But the safe and cozy world of the suburban fifties developed a faith in the goodness of humanity, which in turn led to the "radical moral individualism" of the sixties (16)—the do-your-own-thing "me generation" who rebelled against the least assertion of any external moral authority.

Add to this mix an increasingly relativistic worldview, in which no one's beliefs are to be challenged or actions restrained, and you end up with a nation of self-centered brats who see themselves as victims of any rule, law, or principle that interferes with their quest for self-fulfillment. I would suggest that radical feminism is a result of these various forces converging with a movement that had already begun to place reason above revelation, in some cases to reject the absolute truth of Scripture altogether. With only human reason to rely on, the less radical feminists seem unable to create a unified voice (e.g., are they for abortion or against it?); so the gender feminists have intimidated nearly every group of leaders in the country with their demands for an amorphous and ill-defined "equality," leading to unwise decisions throughout the culture.

It is not that the problems identified by the modern feminists don't exist, just as real problems existed a century ago; many of them do. Occasional unjust job discrimination still remains; rape and abuse, although apparently decreasing, continue to occur far too often; pop culture's denigration of women is commonplace; genuine sexual harassment is alive and well in some workplaces; even the restless discontent that Friedan describes indeed exists in the lives of many women. However, with no external foundation of truth, no absolute standards by which to judge the problems or discover their causes, secular feminists cannot possibly find viable solutions, or even distinguish between real and imaginary problems. They resort to calling for more laws, demanding unfair advantages for women and unjust constraints on men; they insist that every problem any woman ever encounters can be blamed on the oppression of men, refusing to hold women accountable for the problems they themselves create. And in their blind zeal they create new problems that cannot be solved by their ideology either.

The madness of radical feminism is everywhere. Sexual harassment lawsuits are clearly out of control; abortion-on-demand has given us over thirty million dead babies since *Roe v. Wade*; NOW is currently campaigning against a proposed law that would make taking a minor across a state line for an abortion without parental consent a criminal act; we are moving closer daily to the legal recognition of gay and lesbian "marriages." And while many Christians oppose these radical goals of the gender feminists, still feminism has made inroads into the church as well—the subject of the following chapter.

CHAPTER FOUR

Feminism in the Church

§

As we have seen, while secular feminists point out real problems that women face, they make assumptions that cause them to wrongly analyze the sources of those problems, leading them to "solutions" that only create more problems for the society as a whole, for both men and women. We would expect Christians who are concerned about women's problems in the church and society to have a more accurate analysis of those problems, making assumptions and offering solutions based on a biblical worldview. Those who call themselves "biblical feminists" or "egalitarians" claim to do this. Unlike the secular feminists, they profess belief in the foundational doctrines of creation, original sin, and redemption; they also acknowledge that the God of the Bible works personally in the lives of believers. They avoid the strident tone of so many radical feminists, their reasoned discourse reflecting their sincerity.

Many of the early feminists also held to these Christian beliefs. They, however, lived in an era when the Judeo-Christian worldview prevailed and therefore accepted many of the traditional functional differences between men and women. In particular, they highly valued marriage and motherhood, asking for legal equity for protection rather than for massive societal changes. A significant few of those early feminists, however, were also concerned with equality in the church and argued that women should be allowed to hold ecclesiastical teaching and leadership positions. Their arguments, and those of feminists in the church today, are disturbingly similar to those of the modern secular feminists. Rather than beginning with Scripture and assessing the status of women by its truth, they begin with the same major assumptions of their secular counterparts and assess Scripture by these, in the process challenging both the inspiration and inerrancy of the Word. As a result, they offer to the church merely another version of secular feminism veneered with questionable Christian doctrine.

Along with the secular feminists, feminists in the church assume that men and women are equal in every sense of the word; there is no differentiation between them that would demand or allow for a hierarchy of male leadership and female submission, which they assume to be a relationship of superiority and inferiority. (This is where the term *egalitarian* comes in.) This assumption correlates with two other important assumptions. One is that there are no essential, innate differences between men and women beyond reproductive biology; so any apparent personality or emotional differences are solely a result of acculturation based on our sin nature and should be changed when we are redeemed. The other assumption is that men have created an unjust patriarchal system for the purpose of oppressing women and keeping them from fulfilling themselves in meaningful work in the world (i.e., women are victims of men's power).

Feminists in the church, like their secular counterparts, do bring to our attention problems that women face in our culture. While secular feminists, because they reject traditional religion, focus their attention on social problems in the culture at large, egalitarians warn us that the same problems exist within the church. The divorce rate is the same within the Christian community as without; spouse and child abuse occurs at much the same rate; women are often not given opportunities to exercise their gifts for the edification of the church; Christian men are often domineering and/or demeaning in their attitudes toward women; Christian fathers spend too little time with their children. The temptation, often, is to see the absurdity of the radical secular feminists and deny that there is validity to any complaint about the relationships of men and women; thus those who bring the complaints to our attention are to be commended for taking that risk and responsibility.

And egalitarians, as the secular feminists cannot, correctly point out that the root cause of the problems is sin, thus offering the possibility of finding viable solutions. As Mary Stewart Van Leeuwen, a psychologist and professor at Calvin College, explains in *Gender and Grace*, the sinful behaviors of men and women go far deeper than worldly psychology can fathom or help: "[Psychologists] do not realize (or refuse to admit) that something much deeper is at work: something that cannot finally be eradicated by psychotherapy or institutional change" (47).

Van Leeuwen, of course, is profoundly correct; sin is at the heart of all relationship problems. Yet even her assessment of the particular sinful propensities of men and women is predicated on questionable assumptions concerning their pre-Fall equality. From Genesis 1 she identifies two main traits of newly created mankind that relate particularly to our understanding of gender problems—their inherent sociability (God creates both "male and female" in His image; He is also a plural being who exists in fellowship) and their "accountable dominion" (they are given the command to exercise responsible dominion over the earth).

She then claims there is "no indication in the creation accounts that the man was to take the lead in this process" (42). From Genesis 1:28, she notes that both are given the command to exercise dominion; thus, she says, they are to do so as undifferentiated equals, neither one leading or following the other.

In Genesis it is indeed clear that both the man and the woman are to exercise dominion over the earth. The purposes of the two creation accounts differ, however. Genesis 1 is an overview of the entire creation, while Genesis 2 gives us the details of the particular creation of the man and the woman, which Van Leeuwen conveniently skims over. It is in Genesis 2 that the woman is called "a helper suitable for" the man (v. 18, NASB), which at least implies a hierarchy in their relationship. But even before the woman's creation, another event makes the man's leadership yet clearer: God forms the man, places him in the Garden, then—before bringing the animals to him and finally creating the woman—gives the *man* the responsibility to tend the Garden and the command not to eat of the tree of the knowledge of good and evil. Nowhere in Genesis 1 is the command about the tree even hinted at; so it seems obvious that God gave it to the man with the understanding that he would communicate it to the woman, thus taking responsibility from the first for the spiritual welfare of the family. The sequence also suggests the expectation that the man would pass on to the woman the nature of their responsibilities in the Garden, making him responsible for their physical welfare as well.

While ignoring the rest of the Genesis 2 account, Van Leeuwen makes much of the fact that the word "helper" used to describe the woman is the same word used for God when He helps man. This, she believes, means that the man and the woman must have been undifferentiated equals. After all, if we place the woman in a "secondary position" to man because she was created to be a "helper," we must then be placing God in a secondary position to man when we use the word to describe Him. However, the point of calling God our "helper" is not to call on our position relative to His; He is not equal to us either. Rather, it shows His graciousness to willingly and voluntarily accept our request for help to accomplish a task we cannot accomplish alone. This is the same task of the woman in the Garden—not that the man has the right to lord it over her or that she cannot have ideas and work of her own, but she is the one who will, as a norm, willingly and voluntarily come to the aid of the man as he tends the Garden and exercises leadership in the family, helping him fulfill the responsibilities for which he will be held accountable.

Yet another indication of Adam's leadership responsibility occurs in Genesis 3 as God asks for an account of their disobedience. He speaks first to Adam, even though Eve sinned first, and rebukes Adam for listening to Eve's voice (v. 17) instead of obeying Him. And in Romans 5:12-21 we are told that sin entered the race through Adam, not Eve. How could this be unless Adam had been given the responsibility for spiritual leadership, which he then failed to exercise?

This issue of whether man's leadership is given in the Garden, before the Fall, is of immense importance in understanding the nature of man and woman, as Van Leeuwen correctly realizes. If indeed God did not mean for a hierarchy to exist within the family, then those of us who teach it today are incorrect. Van Leeuwen claims that hierarchy is a result of the Fall, not a condition of creation. The primary sin she attributes to the man is the abuse of his "accountable dominion": As a result of the Fall, "there will be a propensity in men to let their dominion run wild, to impose it in cavalier and illegitimate ways not only on earth and on other men, but also upon the person who is bone of his

bones and flesh of his flesh. . . . Legitimate, accountable dominion all too easily becomes male domination" (45).

It is important to remember that this description only covers
a particular manifestation of the sin nature—one that tends to
be more true of men than of women. The sin nature shows itself
in every area of our lives, not just in our relationships to the
opposite sex. And we can all point to examples of men who are
not aggressive but rather sin in their relationships to women by
a passive rejection of the leadership responsibilities God has
given them. However, although Van Leeuwen perhaps goes too
far in ascribing "domination" to all men as their "primary" sinful propensity, her analysis does ring true to some degree. Not
only does experience bear this out—we can all point to examples of overly aggressive, power-hungry men—but so do many
commands we find given to men throughout Scripture.

Men are told in Proverbs, for example, not to chase after
whores but for each to love the wife of his youth; severe penalties are given in the law for rape; Malachi tells men that God
hates divorce. The New Testament confirms that men tend
toward domination by its commands to husbands: "Love your
wives, just as Christ also loved the church and gave Himself for
her" (Eph. 5:25); "So husbands ought to love their own wives
as their own bodies; he who loves his wife loves himself. For no
one ever hated his own flesh, but nourishes and cherishes it, just
as the Lord does the church" (Eph. 5:28-29); "Husbands, love
your wives and do not be bitter toward them" (Col. 3:19). These
exhortations to love show both that men do have a tendency
toward self-centered domination (there is no need to command
people to do what is natural to them) and that leadership con-
sists of loving sacrifice. As Christ is our Head, yet sacrificed
Himself for us, so men are to be willing to lay down their lives
for those whom God calls them to lead. Therefore, men need to

curb any sinful desire for power over others and learn to rely on God's grace to instead be sacrificial leaders.

But Van Leeuwen's assessment of what she calls woman's primary sin as a result of the Fall carries less credence. She says that woman's tendency is to abuse the sociability God created us for by using "the preservation of . . . relationships as an excuse not to exercise accountable dominion in the first place." Woman's flaw, in other words, is "the temptation to avoid taking risks that might upset relationships." She will do anything to maintain peace, including being silent when she should speak up about sinful behavior and refusing to develop "personal self-sufficiency," all so she can preserve even "pathological relationships with the opposite sex" (46).

Certainly this tendency does exist. I can no longer count the number of women students I've had who have experienced abusive relationships that they often tried to maintain beyond any rational hope that they would "work." Yet, is this the "primary" sin that has affected all women since the Fall? I'm not convinced.

For one thing, my own experience tells me that more women—unbelievers as well as believers—do *not* have this tendency than do. Furthermore, the idea that it is sinful to "avoid developing self-sufficiency" (by which Van Leeuwen apparently means to create a career and a personal life that give a woman complete independence) is based on the questionable assumption that men and women are undifferentiated equals, and husbands therefore should not be expected to support their wives; wives should share equally in the economic support of the family and should not depend in any way on their husbands. Yet many contented women do not have careers outside the home, and their husbands are glad to take the responsibility of providing for them as they concentrate on raising the children, making the home a comfortable place to live, and ministering to others in a variety of ways.

But I find it most disturbing that Van Leeuwen casts as woman's primary sinful tendency that which she does to herself, not what she does to others. This suggests an assumption that women are primarily victims of the Fall, and that they are invariably victims of the men in their lives—another questionable assumption from secular feminism. However, these are assumptions not supported by scriptural evidence. Of course women are at times victims of men. However, men are at times victims of women too. Men may seduce women, but women just as often seduce men; the many admonitions in Proverbs to stay away from the adulterous woman tell us this. And I don't see commands directed in Scripture to women that instruct them to "develop self-sufficiency." Rather, women are commanded to "submit to [their] own husbands, as is fitting in the Lord" (Col. 3:18; Eph. 5:22) and to see to it that they respect their husbands (Eph. 5:33). Older women are to admonish the younger women, among other things, to be "obedient to their own husbands, that the word of God may not be blasphemed" (Titus 2:4-5).

These commands given to women in Scripture, and many of its examples, suggest that instead of a failure to develop self-sufficiency, women may have a sinful tendency to desire power and control that are not legitimately theirs. This of course is only one manifestation of the sin nature; as with men, women will show their sinfulness in many varied ways. But this seems to be a general tendency in their relationships to men. In Scripture we see this again and again. Jezebel is an obvious example of a woman whose desire for power leads her to horrendous sinful behavior. Michal's disrespect for David's spiritual leadership earns her barrenness. Rebekah's deceitful preemption of Isaac's authority results in Jacob's having to flee for his life. Delilah's desire for power leads to Samson's loss of spiritual authority as she seduces his secret from him.

Look once again at the creation story. If we assume the man's responsibility is to lead and the woman's is to be his helper, the actions of each at the Fall suggest a different interpretation from Van Leeuwen's. The woman listens to the serpent's theological argument, is deceived by it, takes the fruit, and offers it to the man—thus taking the spiritual leadership given to him. The man, listening silently to the argument and undeceived by it, takes the fruit from the woman, thus reneging on his responsibility for the spiritual welfare of them both, as well as their offspring. Eve was deceived, we are told; Adam was not (1 Tim. 2:14). Thus he retained clarity of mind and spirit and could have intervened, pleading with and protecting his wife, and perhaps averting the entire disaster—at the least, not sinning himself.

We can look, too, at God's judgment on their sin for further evidence that role reversal was at the heart of the Fall. First, Adam's responsibility to provide for his family will become harder; instead of a pleasurable, simple task to delight in, it will cost him hard, sweaty labor. Eve's task of childbearing will similarly entail pain and sorrow it would not have in Eden. The second part of God's judgment on Eve is the most significant: "Your desire shall be for your husband, and he shall rule over you." Van Leeuwen takes "desire" here to mean she will desire his companionship so much that she will sin to gain it. However, the term is an unusual one, used only one other time in Scripture. In Genesis 4:6 we find this statement of God to Cain: "Sin lies at the door. And its *desire* is for you, but you should rule over it." The term *desire* here means "long to rule over" or "dominate"; sin longed to dominate Cain and bring him under its control. Thus, when God tells Eve her "desire" will be for Adam, He is saying she will wish to rule over or dominate him—which she was not created to do. Cain is told that he "should *rule over* [sin]"—overcome or master it, and Eve is told that Adam "shall *rule over*" her. Again, the same words are used here, saying that despite her desire for domination, Adam will remain her head. Of course, the sin nature now guarantees that this headship will not always be through sacrificial love, and the stage is set for the battle of the sexes that still rages today.

This interpretation does not require that the woman be more easily deceived than the man, as some claim. The serpent did not necessarily choose to speak to her for that reason; if he could get the couple to overthrow their basic vocation of gender, he could ensure trouble between them for all time. This he most effectively accomplished by enticing Eve to take the lead.

This view of the Fall—the created hierarchy of leadership and submission being reversed—then makes perfect sense of the New Testament passages that Van Leeuwen calls "ambiguous" and that all egalitarians call into question in some significant way. When Paul says that women are not to teach or hold authority over men in the church, he is instructing us to make a public demonstration of man's spiritual leadership. When he instructs women to submit to their husbands, he is upholding the creation order of the man's responsibility for the spiritual and physical welfare of his family.

As we look at some of these passages more closely, we will do well to think of what Ron Rhodes, president of Reasoning from the Scriptures Ministries, says: "We gain perspective on this issue by recognizing that the biblical world view is based on the assumption that a personal God sovereignly designed an orderly universe to function in a particular way. Crucial to this world view is the concept of authority." Are we, men and women alike, willing to submit to His authority in the matter of how He designed us?

First Timothy 2:11-14 says, "Let a woman learn in silence with all submission. And I do not permit a woman to teach or to have authority over a man, but to be in silence. For Adam was formed first, then Eve. And Adam was not deceived, but the woman being deceived, fell into transgression." Paul is discussing behavior in the church meetings: Men are to pray in confidence; women are to focus on learning instead of teaching. The instruction on silence cannot be a total prohibition from speech, as Paul condones women's praying and prophesying as long as they wear a head covering (1 Cor. 11:5). Here, however, he places a particular restriction on women's public speech: They are not to teach men or hold authority over them. In other words, the public teaching ministry of the church is to be the men's, as is the church's authoritative administration. Women are to listen in silence to the teaching of the elders, with an attitude of obedience to what they hear.

Paul appeals to the creation order as the basis of this command, strengthening the sense of Adam's leadership and responsibility: He was formed first, so he was to be the leader, and man's leadership in the church is a public demonstration of this order. Women should thus not teach men in the meetings, as a public testimony to their position of submission. The statement does not say that women are more easily deceived than men and thus can't teach. It rather implies they are to be in submission because *when Eve took over Adam's role*, she was deceived and fell into sin. Women can teach women and children, and we know that Priscilla participated with her husband in teaching Apollos "the way of God more accurately" (Acts 18:26). Why would these activities be allowed and even commanded (commended in Priscilla's case) if women are more easily deceived than men? The church is the public testimony to the world of

God's order; if we do not follow that order, both we and others will be led astray by our disobedience.

Understanding this passage helps us understand Paul's command in 1 Corinthians 14:34-35: "Let your women keep silent in the churches, for they are not permitted to speak; but they are to be submissive, as the law also says. And if they want to learn something, let them ask their own husbands at home; for it is shameful for women to speak in church." At first glance, this appears to be an all-inclusive command—no woman should ever say a word in the church meetings. However, 1 Corinthians 11 at least allows for women to pray and prophesy, as we have seen. Assuming the inspired Word does not contradict itself, we must take these verses in chapter 14 to mean a certain *kind* of speech, available to us through the context.

Paul has just been giving instruction on how to conduct the act of prophesying in the public meetings. More than one prophet would most likely speak, and other prophets would judge their words—explain and correct them if necessary. In keeping with 1 Corinthians 11 and recalling the creation context of leadership and submission in 1 Timothy 2, it appears that women could prophesy, but they could not publicly judge the words of other prophets, since such judgment would entail teaching, which the Timothy passage proscribes. It could also be seen as a public challenge to male authority, which would be shameful for women. Instead, they were to take up any questions about another prophet's words with their husbands in the privacy of the home.

When he writes of the marriage relationship, Paul reiterates the same message through a different picture: The relationship of man to woman is one of leadership and submission by definition and from creation. In Ephesians 5:25 and following, Paul commands men to love their wives as Christ loves the church, and women to submit to their husbands *because* Christ is the head of the church. Obviously, Christ holds leadership authority over the church, which submits to Him; husbands and wives reflect that status not because of the perversion of equal status at the Fall, surely, but because we were originally created as leader and helpmeet. This Paul affirms in 1 Corinthians 11: "The head of every man is Christ, the head of woman is man, and the head of Christ is God" (v. 3). "For man is not from woman, but woman from man. Nor was man created for the woman, but woman for the man" (vv. 8-9).

Only in the context of a created order of leadership and submission can these passages be clearly understood, which is why they appear ambiguous to egalitarians, who deny that order. Part of the problem is their flawed view of hierarchy. They assume that a hierarchy requires that the leader be considered superior and the follower inferior. Certainly there are those in leadership positions who act as though this is the case, but common sense tells us otherwise. I am a professor of English at a small Christian college. As such I am under the leadership of, among others, the academic dean. Any decision he makes that affects my actions is binding on me as a condition of my employment. Yet I do not consider myself inferior to him in terms of my personhood, my academic abilities, or my spiritual standing before our Lord. Hierarchy is a way of life; all of us come under various authorities and yet do not consider ourselves inferior to them. Generals direct soldiers, employers direct employees, teachers direct students, police direct citizens. In all cases, the authority is derived foremost from the position; even if I do not respect the person of a leader, I owe respect for the position and submission to all directives that do not require me to sin. I know of no one who claims these hierarchies imply superiority and inferiority. Why do some then claim that hierarchy within the church and family must imply this?

Because they cannot accept that there can be hierarchy without superiority and inferiority, the egalitarians must find a way to deal with these passages of Scripture. Their most important argument is that Galatians 3:28 rids the church and family of all hierarchy: "There is neither Jew nor Greek, there is neither slave nor free, there is neither male nor female; for you are all one in Christ Jesus." But the context of this verse clearly refers to our spiritual standing before God, in which we are all equal and we each stand alone before Him (I cannot stand on my parents' salvation or my husband's; I must receive Christ's sacrifice for myself). Too many instructions are given throughout the New Testament for the exercise of leadership to accept that believers, equal before God, are to have no leaders. In fact, those who claim there is no sexual hierarchy do accept hierarchy within the church—they just want women to be able to exercise leadership as well as men. Yet if hierarchy is right at all, why not sexual hierarchy? If sexual hierarchy implies superiority and inferiority, why not all hierarchy? If hierarchy and its implied superiority and inferiority is really the issue for the egalitarians, why do they call for the positions of leadership that will make them superior to others in the church? Why do they not call instead for abolishing leadership positions altogether?

But if hierarchy is acceptable because leadership is necessary within a community, male leadership in the church and home can also be justified without saying that men are superior to women. True, not all leaders are equipped for or competent at their jobs, and far too many abuse their positions. There are elected officials for whom I have no personal respect; yet I am called to obey them as long as they are not requiring me to sin, even if their directives are not always for the best. The call for male leadership is based on the vocation of gender God gives to all males at conception. All men will not exercise this vocation properly, but it does not follow that no men should ever exercise it, any more than brutality on the part of some police officers causes us to disband all law enforcement agencies. Nor does abuse of male leadership excuse women from exercising their vocation of womanly submission nor for their demanding to exercise the masculine vocation of leadership. Thankfully—and in part as a result of the work of the egalitarians in pointing out problems in the church—there are increasing resources within the Christian community to help couples and individuals who find themselves within relationships where gender vocations are not being exercised according to God's principles.

Mary Kassian, in *The Feminist Gospel: The Movement to Unite Feminism with the Church*, explains how the egalitarian assumption of undifferentiated equality between men and women undermines the inerrancy and inspiration of Scripture. She calls equality the *crux interpretum* of the egalitarians: "They interpreted questionable texts to align with their own understanding of sexual equality, which they defined as monolithic, undifferentiated role-interchangeability" (208). Galatians 3:28, discussed above, becomes the scriptural cornerstone of their argument, and despite the fact that its context does not bear their interpretation, they insist that all other Scripture concerning male and female relationships must give way to it. So, starting from the secular culture's assumption of equality, they have found a proof-text to "support" it and claim that the entire Bible must be aligned with it.

In order, then, to deal with the passages that command a male-female hierarchy in the church and home within this framework, they resort to poor biblical exegesis. Either they claim outright that Scripture contradicts itself and those passages are simply wrong (because of Paul's deeply entrenched patriarchalism) or they resort to tortured readings. Kassian discusses these in somewhat more detail in *Women, Creation, and the Fall*, where she points out several basic rules of interpretation that the egalitarians violate.

As we have already seen, the context of a passage is vital to its clear understanding—a rule the egalitarians ignore in their exegesis of Galatians 3:28. Another error is their insistence on placing incidental passages or examples above doctrinal passages. Because a person named Junias (Junia in the *New King James Version*), who *may* have been female, is said to be "of note among the apostles" (Rom. 16:7), the egalitarians insist that this is an example of female leadership at the highest level. However, the wording is ambiguous and could serve two or three meanings, including merely that the apostles highly regarded her (or him—there is conflicting evidence concerning the person's sex); therefore, the reference must yield to the clear doctrinal teaching of 1 Timothy that women are not to teach or hold authority over men. However we understand the reference, it cannot mean that Junias was a female elder or apostle in the church.

A third problem with the egalitarian exegesis is the use of cultural arguments to dismiss the clear meaning of a passage. If a passage does not support their assumption of equality, they claim it is addressing solely a cultural issue that is no longer relevant. For example, some argue that the restriction on teaching was given merely because women in Paul's day were not well-educated; so the restriction no longer applies. Never mind that nothing in the context could possibly suggest this meaning.

There are other problems with an egalitarian interpretation of Scripture, all of which undermine its authority as the inerrant and inspired Word of God. As Kassian puts it, "Once the possibility of error or cultural conditioning is accepted, how does one determine what parts or principles of Scripture are of abiding authority or value? Human reason ultimately becomes the judge of what is really God's Word and what is not" (*Women*, 154). At their root, these practices reflect the same problem we saw in the early feminist movement: Reason and experience are valued above revelation. In fact, there are few arguments used by today's egalitarians that had not already been posed by certain of the early feminists. The prevailing Judeo-Christian worldview of their era made the difference in how extensive the effects of their thinking became.

The way egalitarians define equality also correlates with the assumption that there are no innate differences between men and women (beyond the purely physical reproductive differences) that would account for or encourage male leadership and female submission. Here they also join some of the early feminists in placing science above Scripture. Van Leeuwen's book, in fact, is almost entirely an overview of studies that appear to prove this point. However, the majority of psychological, biological, and anthropological studies—not to mention experience and common sense, as well as scriptural example—actually do point to innate differences that are difficult to change and appear to create damage when we attempt to do so. (See, for example, Christen and Goldberg.) Every "stereotype" of feminine and masculine behavior does not apply to every woman and man, but most women do naturally and willingly tend toward feminine attitudes and behaviors while most men do naturally and willingly tend toward masculine attitudes and behaviors. Of course, this includes sinful behaviors as well as righteous; both femininity and masculinity can be abused and perverted. But Van Leeuwen would have us believe that the very concepts of femininity and masculinity are the result not of creation but of the Fall.

The other assumption that correlates with the egalitarians'

definition of equality is that patriarchy (male dominance in most aspects of the culture) is an unjust condition imposed by fallen men on women to suppress women's gifts of leadership. Van Leeuwen at least admits that patriarchy is the universal condition of all cultures, unlike some feminists who go to great lengths to "prove" that in some golden past women were in charge of a peaceful and just world. Biblical history, of course, precludes any such golden age, as there were only two inhabitants of Eden—and either Adam was their leader or neither led the other, depending on whether you take the traditionalist or feminist view of creation.

However, Van Leeuwen, along with all other feminists, does assume that patriarchy is by definition unjust and that one goal of Christians—who have been redeemed from the sin nature, which she believes has created patriarchy—must be to create a culture in which men and women are undifferentiated equals. She claims that patriarchy necessarily makes women of "lower social status" than men (113). The precise roles and activities of men and women do vary from culture to culture (except for those constrained by physical differences—childbearing and nursing and activities requiring greater physical strength); but no matter what activities men do in a particular culture, those activities will invariably hold a higher social status. From her own experience, she describes two West African tribes. In the tribe in which men build houses and women make baskets, house building is seen as more important than basket making; in the other, in which women build houses and men make baskets, basket making is seen as more important (113-114).

In her proof of this phenomenon, Van Leeuwen switches from who makes what to who's in power. She quotes two anthropologists who say that no one has ever "observed a society in which women have publicly recognized power and authority surpassing that of men. Everywhere we find that women are excluded from certain crucial economic or political activities, that their roles as wives and mothers are associated with fewer powers and prerogatives than the roles of men" (quoted on 114 [see notes 8-9, p. 261]). We have seen this concern elsewhere. It bothers secular feminists a great deal that men's work appears to carry more prestige and power; that's the real reason they want "equal opportunities" for *all* jobs and cry "discrimination" when there aren't enough female CEOs to satisfy their sense of "justice."

Then Van Leeuwen turns to a discussion of patriarchy in the church. After claiming that most of the metaphors describing the Christian life derive from feminine activities such as birth, nurturing, and serving—conveniently ignoring many metaphors of men's work such as farming, construction, warfare, and sports—Van Leeuwen says that this is why many men will not even consider the claims of the Gospel, because Christianity requires them to debase themselves to the lower status of women. She then hypothesizes (saying that it is not possible to find this out because it is subconscious or denied) that because of this conflict between their idea of manliness and the need to become more feminized to follow Christ, Christian men have turned churches into "thorough hierarchical structures, with women kept as low in the hierarchy as possible." Men, she says, delegate the "nurturing" tasks (nursery duty, food services, etc.) to women and keep for themselves the "more formal, visible, and well-paid tasks—theologizing, preaching, the making of important administrative decisions." Then she further claims they have created a special jargon and training for themselves in order to be further distanced from women, and finally she accuses men of becoming "quite authoritarian" in the home to somehow maintain their manliness despite being Christian (118-119).

I find this assessment of patriarchy fascinating. The more I have read in the literature of the egalitarians, the more I am struck with their assumption—paralleling that of the secular feminists once again—that the "higher status" work of men is to be *preferred* to the work of women, that men must be protecting their fragile egos by conspiring to keep women out of the public eye. They accept that social status, prestige, and power are the most important values for Christians to strive for, just as they are the most important values of the world. Yet, God says that only the one who loses himself will be fulfilled on earth and honored in eternity. Jesus reminded His disciples of this principle by telling them that their leaders should not "lord it over" them but must be servants and slaves to those they lead, serving and sacrificing as He did (Matt. 20:25-28). And He reminded them that God is the One who exalts; just as a guest ought to seat himself in the lowest place at the table and let the host place him higher (Luke 14:7-11), we should choose the lowliest attitude, that of a servant, if we desire to be leaders. This is not the way of the world.

Still more troubling is that Van Leeuwen asserts that men's striving after status and prestige and power is the result of their sinful nature, and yet she wants women to have status, prestige, and power too. Surely she doesn't desire for women to change from one sinful propensity to another? Her assessment of women's sinful nature does help her to hide this contradiction, perhaps even from herself: If men and women are not different, and if women's sin is a refusal of self-sufficiency and our work in the world, then it makes sense that we should try to become more like men. However, if women's actual sinful tendency is to desire inappropriate power and leadership, Van Leeuwen shows us that very nature—with the sheep's clothing of the rationalization of biblical truth.

If Van Leeuwen were correct about male-female hierarchy

being a result of the Fall, one would expect to see somewhere, at least within the Christian community, a successful example of an egalitarian society. Yet there has never been such; even when feminists point to women of prominence in the Bible or in church history, there is little to no evidence that these women were actually functioning as elders and teachers and theologians. In fact, the question Van Leeuwen poses more than once is telling: Why do women just put up with being oppressed and demeaned by men? To claim that women are sinning by "accepting a subordinate status" in society makes little sense, considering the highly independent, self-centered pride that mars every human being's character.

But in fact it is the constant frustrated complaint of feminists everywhere that women just don't seem to understand what's good for them. Women are the greatest enemies of this equality the feminists demand. Can it really be because they are content to live in degradation or are so afraid of men that they cower in fear of even thinking of "liberation" from their degraded status? What a low view of their sisters! No wonder they themselves tend to denigrate all who choose a traditional role, for the more who do so, the greater the threat becomes to feminism itself.

David J. Ayers, a sociology professor at Dallas Baptist University, offers a most enlightening example of an attempt at a truly egalitarian society: the Israeli kibbutz. The kibbutz was organized specifically to obliterate as many gender roles as possible; large families were discouraged; living space was "adequate" but not spacious so that less time need be spent on housekeeping chores; day care was provided; and all roles other than childbirth were assigned without regard to sex—in particular, women were strongly encouraged to be active in careers and politics. And the women who were a part of the kibbutz were there voluntarily, desiring to establish this "unisex" environment.

It sounds like, and was designed to be, a feminist heaven—and as such it failed. It did not fail because the men of the kibbutz began taking over the roles of power and prestige and insisting that the women take lesser roles. It failed because the *women* of the kibbutz demanded more time to spend with their children, as well as larger homes and more time to spend tending them, preferring to do the work in the home themselves rather than allow their husbands to help them. The persistence of men in offering them high-status occupations and discouraging them from having children did not alter their decisions; women turned down work and political opportunities even when they were better qualified than men in order to spend more time in domestic affairs—just as more and more women in corporate America are quitting their high-paid, prestigious positions to raise their children themselves. One kibbutz woman remarked to someone surprised by this outcome of the experiment, "Why is it all so surprising? What did you expect women to do?" (quoted on 320).

Could it be that masculinity and femininity are not results of the Fall, but innate attributes of our very humanity that lead us to prefer certain activities for very good reasons—reasons stemming from God's creation of a man to lead and protect and provide and a woman to come alongside him to serve and nurture?

Van Leeuwen rightly says that neither the egalitarians nor the complementarians (those who hold the traditional view that the sexes complement each other in their differing functions) should "dismiss or caricature the concerns of the other" if we wish to have helpful dialogue on the relationships of men and women (239). She then proceeds to not so subtly caricature what she calls in various places the "subordinationist" or "anti-liberationist" view. Although she acknowledges there are differences in opinion on the exact meaning and scope of male leadership, she takes the most extreme view—that it means all women are to be subordinate to all men in all circumstances—and claims that anyone who believes in male leadership must hold that view or be inconsistent in his or her beliefs.

I must assume there are such extremists, though I have never encountered them. It is a view that would indeed be almost impossible to live by. How, for example, could a mother discipline her son if she is to be subordinate to him? Or what if her male pastor asks her to do an activity that her husband does not want her to do? However, it is hardly fair to use this extreme to characterize all who believe in male leadership, especially when many such believers have made cogent and logical arguments for limited leadership—husbands of wives and male elders in teaching and administration of the church—based clearly on Scripture. This view allows immense freedom for women to exercise their gifts in the home, the church, and society at large (a freedom, it is sadly true, that too many churches do not nurture).

The creation of man and woman was the creation of human society—with the family as its cornerstone. If Adam is given responsibility in the family to lead spiritually, provide physically, and protect its members, Eve is created to be his partner, lovingly coming alongside him to help him carry out his responsibilities and with the special work of serving and nurturing the family—including leadership roles in relation to the children and servants of the family. This becomes a model for the family in particular. Applying this model to the broader society takes extreme care, I think. Aside from some minimal specific restrictions within the church and family, Scripture does not directly address woman's particular roles. The innate masculinity and femininity of individuals, however, make the patriarchal society a predictable outcome. Men will gravitate toward roles of leadership, protection, and provision, while women will gravitate toward roles of nurturing and serving.

This, however, does not mean that all women must be submissive to all men without distinction. Neither in the Old or New Testament do we have examples of such universal female submission, and the New Testament commands concerning Christian women are clearly addressed solely to their position within church and family. Male leadership, in other words, is commanded solely within the family and the church but, because of the innate differences between men and women, will tend to be a general trend in society as a whole. Many studies show that more women do not hold high-paying, high-profile jobs for the simple reason that not many women want them; women who must work tend to prefer jobs that allow them the most time and energy to devote to family matters.

However, to say that women *cannot* be leaders of any sort within society is going beyond the teaching of Scripture. I know that for myself I would be uncomfortable holding even a college department headship, though I enjoy administering a writing center staffed by students. I have seen women, however, in administrative positions who are comfortable and efficient, without losing any of their femininity, and who have the complete respect and cooperation of the men they supervise. In fact, Scripture abounds with examples of women as employers. The Proverbs 31 woman supervises servants in both household and field work; Sarah had complete control over Hagar; Lydia, apparently the single head of a household and a businesswoman, undoubtedly employed a number of workers. Nothing in Scripture, in other words, says that women can't ever be leaders and employers over men; the only constraints are within the marriage relationship and the church.

And Scripture does give clear instruction for male leadership within the church. Man's spiritual leadership is his most crucial responsibility, for it involves the eternal souls of his family members. Adam's refusal of that responsibility in the Garden of Eden led not just to his death but to the deaths of all humanity after him. And so within the church we are instructed that men should lead and teach—not because men are better than women or less likely to be deceived than women or because women are not gifted in these areas, but because men are primarily responsible for spiritual leadership, and God wants them to publicly fulfill that responsibility as a demonstration of it to believers and unbelievers alike.

This restriction on women's teaching and leading is actually quite minimal, however, as it applies solely within the public meetings and the administration of the church. As John Piper points out in "A Vision of Biblical Complementarity: Manhood and Womanhood Defined According to the Bible," women still have many ministries open to them. Women gifted as teachers may teach in children's, youths', and women's Sunday school classes, in private or public schools, in a neighborhood Bible study, in radio and speaking ministries aimed toward women. In fact, they may teach any subject to anyone that is not "authoritative doctrinal teaching" (Moo, 185), and they may teach doctrine to other women and to children. Women gifted in administration may work in any number of ministries within the church and society: ministries to the sick, the handicapped, the socially estranged, prison ministries, sports ministries, women's ministries, drama and radio ministries, etc. (Piper, 58). So long as they are not in authority over men in the church setting, any administrative position appears to be open to women, including administration within the church that does not involve the pastoral authority defined in 1 Timothy 3:5 and 5:17 (Moo, 187).

When we consider how few teaching and pastoral positions are even needed in comparison to the amount of work to be done in the church, then add all the work outside the church that women are free to engage in, it is hard to sympathize with the complaint that women are too restricted. (I realize some individual churches are too restrictive, but this is a wrong that should be righted without throwing out clear doctrine.) Apparently the egalitarians have indeed joined their secular counterparts in assessing value by standards of prestige and pay. Van Leeuwen even says that women must share the economic load of the family to have self-worth, and since industrialization removed much "meaningful" (i.e., obviously economically helpful) work from the home, women must now be allowed to pursue careers—because to focus on childrearing "fosters economic dependence and isolates [mothers] from other adults" (200).

I would agree that industrialization did away with much of the work that made homemaking a true challenge and a creative venture. But does this by necessity mean that a full-time wife and mother is a "leech" on her husband, as many feminists claim, and has no contact with adults? Only if she chooses a lifestyle that denies the feminine mandate of her Lord to be a servant.

A woman without a paying job is hardly a leech. In the merely practical sense, she is doing the housework that would otherwise be dcne by a paid employee, and many homemakers save money and nurture their family's health and creativity through such ventures as breadmaking, sewing, and a multitude of economizing measures. Certainly my mother has contributed in these ways to the ability she and my father have to travel and to help out their children and grandchildren and community in their retirement. And the time-saving devices and prepared foods and store-bought clothing that we all enjoy simply leave more time for other kinds of ministry work within the neighborhood, church, and community.

However, even more importantly, the woman who is a full-time wife and mother offers a true reflection of one aspect of the mystery that marriage is made to suggest: the relationship between Christ and the church. Christ has done all the giving; the church has done all the receiving. The good works of the church are not accomplished to pay back the Lord for His work of salvation, but to express our love and gratefulness to Him for His work. In a small way, a woman's work in her family, if done out of gratefulness for the sacrifices her husband makes in supporting and leading them, reflects this particular aspect of the church's relationship to its Lord.

Neither does a woman without a paying job need to be isolated from adult contact, even while raising very young children. I recall well the busyness and frustrations of raising four children born within five and a half years; but I was never isolated from adults during that time, despite being naturally introverted. My neighbors, my Christian sisters, my extended family all were important to me during those years and challenged me as well to reach out to others so that no young mother was left without fellowship for extended periods. And being a full-time wife and mother certainly doesn't mean a woman can't be involved in a variety of ministries outside her home, as her gifts and her family responsibilities allow. I can't count the number of happily "unemployed" women I know—including my mother and her friends—who have been busy and fulfilled throughout the various stages of their lives without pay or public recognition but with the highest praise of their husbands and children and many, many others influenced by their godly service.

This, it finally seems to me, is the heart of the issue. Egalitarians like Van Leeuwen have rightly seen the abuse of male leadership in society, the church, and the family, but have sought to analyze it beginning with modern secular assumptions about men and about women. These wrong assumptions lead to what certainly begins to sound like jealousy (called "seeking justice") as they insist that women be allowed to exercise the same leadership roles as men. As Elisabeth Elliot puts it in "The Essence of Femininity," "Listening to a good many solemn dialogues on the roles of women in this or that or the other thing, I noticed that 'this or that or the other thing' was never anything to do with fishing or farming or writing a book or giving birth to a baby, but always something that touched in some way on questions of authority or power or competition or money" (395).

But this solution—to place women in the same power and prestige positions as men—has proven invalid in the secular society, where women granted equal status remain discontented, demanding yet more "rights," becoming increasingly hostile to men, seeking fulfillment through increasingly desperate avenues of promiscuity, false religion, and lesbianism. The church has the opportunity to offer the true solution to the battle of the sexes; but we must all, men and women alike, be willing to accept Jesus' call to serve and not to be served (see Mark 10:45). The church needs to affirm women's giftedness and help women find appropriate ministry for the use of their gifts in the church and in the world, at the same time helping and affirming those women who choose to be full-time wives and mothers to understand their deeply significant value to the church and to the world. The church must deny, emphatically and publicly, that men are better than women and prove that they mean it: first, by refusing to glamorize leadership and emphasizing the sacrificial stewardship necessary for true service in such positions, and, second, by recognizing and celebrating women's unique vocation and unique contributions. And the church must at the same time insist that God's design, evident from creation, is the only way any of us will find fulfillment—men in sacrificial leadership and women in nurturing service.

CHAPTER FIVE

The Call to Womanhood

🌀

Feminism fails because it wrongly identifies the source of the problems women face in today's culture. The claim that men and women are functionally equivalent leads to the conclusion that men have—consciously or subconsciously—conspired to create a social system that prevents women from achieving full status and dignity as human beings. Add to this the worship of prestige and wealth, and of course it appears unfair that mostly men hold positions of leadership and power in our society.

However, attempts to restructure the society along gender-neutral lines are failing miserably and, in fact, creating more problems than they were meant to solve.

A different perspective is needed, a perspective found in God's love letter to His created children. Men need to embrace the ideal of manhood as given in Scripture and obey God's commands to love and cherish their wives and to respect all women. Women need to embrace the ideal of womanhood as given in Scripture and obey God's commands to respect and submit to their husbands and to behave in a womanly fashion at all times, whether married or single.

It isn't a matter of figuring out what men want us to be or what other women want us to be or what we in our sinful flesh want to be; it's a matter of figuring out what God intends us to be. And the first thing He created each of us to be was either male or female, giving us the vocation of our sex, as Martin Luther might call it. (The source of Martin Luther's ideas presented here is Gustaf Wingren's *Luther on Vocation*.)

Vocation (or "calling"), according to Luther, is that which we are and do in relation to our neighbors. It has nothing to do with our relationship to God in regard to securing our salvation or His approval. Nor is vocation merely career, in Luther's definition. Rather, it is any station one holds in life. Thus, family relationships are vocations—I am daughter, wife, and mother; as are social relations—I am neighbor, church member, consumer, friend; and occupations—I am writer, employee, administrator, teacher. "In anything that involves action, anything that concerns the world or my relationship with my neighbor, there is nothing, Luther holds, that falls in a private sphere by lying outside of . . . vocation" (Wingren, 5). We are bound to others in relationship in all our earthly doings.

Even those who don't know God act for the benefit of others through vocation. It is vocation, Luther maintains, that keeps us from acting entirely on our selfish desires and creates the orderly community God desires on earth. Parents, for example, generally provide for their family economically and try to assure a decent future for their children by educating them and/or training them for a trade. People in government and law enforcement generally work to protect the citizens and maintain a peaceful environment. Workers ply their trades, whether shoemaking or software development, to provide goods and jobs for others. Even selfish desires for economic security and social respect generally ensure that vocation will create a certain amount of order in a society.

Vocation, then, pressures even unbelievers to at least outwardly obey the second commandment—to love our neighbors as ourselves—and to maintain a relatively peaceful and moral environment. For the Christian, of course, our actions toward our neighbors are motivated by our love for them, which is founded in our love for God. We do not earn God's approval through loving our neighbors; He loves them through us as we act for their good in accordance with His character. We no longer serve our neighbors from duty only, but from genuine desire. "Love does not think about doing works, it finds joy in people," Wingren explains; "love never does something because it has to" (43).

The first vocational distinction, the one created in the Garden, is our sex; by virtue of birth I am called to be a woman. Elisabeth Elliot writes, "We sometimes hear the expression 'the accident of sex,' as though one's being a man or a woman were a triviality. It is very far from being a triviality. It is our nature. It is the modality under which we live all our lives; it is what you and I are called to be—called by God, this God who is in charge. It is our destiny, planned, ordained, fulfilled by an all-wise, all-powerful, all-loving Lord" (*Let Me*, 17).

I can neither choose nor escape this vocation, though I may attempt to ignore or deny some of its particular responsibilities. Being a woman necessarily governs every relationship I have. It does not require that I marry and have children—though most women do—but it does mean that I will perceive and think and act in ways that are "womanly," as opposed to "manly." My actions toward my neighbors—parents, colleagues, friends, husband, children—all begin in my birth identity as woman.

"Just treat me like a human being," many women say. And

in some regards, this may be a sound desire. Spiritually, there is no distinction between male and female in our relationship with God; we are all heirs equally in Christ. This would suggest that all relational principles for believers apply equally to men and to women: loving one another, putting others first, rebuking and restoring those who sin, and so on. There may also be a place in the world for the sentiment "just treat me like a human being"; the early feminists fought for laws that did not privilege women over men but merely gave them the same reasonable legal rights as men already had.

However, the sex of another person is not something that can be so easily passed over in our daily relationships. For one thing, our experience alone tells us we are different. Many times a male colleague has looked at my mystified or appalled expression and assured me, "It's a man thing." Often something that appears perfectly logical to me draws only a blank stare and a shake of the head from my husband. Consistently when "stereotypical" portraits of men or women come up in my college classes, these very modern young adults groan or laugh and say, "That is so true!"

An impromptu survey in my freshman classes at a Christian college, in which I asked students to list traits they considered to be "feminine" or "masculine," netted an interesting consistency. Women were described again and again as "emotional, sensitive, motherly, nurturing, caring, compassionate." Men consistently received adjectives such as "strong, tough, steadfast, logical, competitive, aggressive."

Surely no one would seriously claim that women can't be logical or aggressive or that men can't be sensitive or compassionate. Yet it seems true to experience that men and women naturally tend toward certain character traits that most people agree on, generally something like the lists my freshmen gave me. Some prefer to think of these traits as culturally conditioned (Van Leeuwen is of this thinking, for example). However, let's revisit the creation account and see how the qualities we think of as "masculine" and "feminine" grow out of the purposes for which Adam and Eve were created.

The creation of Adam before Eve does not in any way, as we have noted, imply superiority. Both, in the Genesis 1 account, are given dominion over the earth and all that is in it. However, the creation order does imply Adam's position as leader and initiator. In Genesis 2, in fact, as we have seen, the command concerning the tree of knowledge is given to Adam before Eve is created, suggesting his responsibility to lead spiritually. Also, Adam's naming of the animals denotes his leadership over creation, just as his giving the generic name "woman" to Eve denotes his leadership in the family. He is created also with a specific physical responsibility: to tend and keep the Garden God has created and thus provide for his family.

Eve's creation never ceases to awe me. For the first time in the days of His creating, God sees something that is "not good"—the man has no companion. The animals cannot fill his need for help or fellowship; so God creates a woman. Not from the dust of the ground, as Adam was created, but from a portion of Adam's actual physical body; she is literally a part of him, and they are literally one flesh. Her purpose is to fill Adam's need for a companion and to be a helper "comparable to" or "suitable for" (NIV, NASB) him—one who could come alongside him in his responsibilities and help him fulfill them.

To be a "suitable" helper is certainly not to be inferior. As discussed in Chapter 4, Eve's role as helper must be seen as the role of one who willingly and voluntarily shares in the task at hand in order to make it easier for the one responsible, not as that of a servant to be ordered about for the pleasure and convenience of a master. Neither does the role of helper suggest that a woman is meant to live her years barefoot, pregnant, and in the kitchen. A quick glance through Proverbs 31 should dispel any notion that even a married woman with children can't exercise many vocations besides wife, mother, and housekeeper.

This account of creation can help us explore manhood and womanhood. It is true that even those of us who agree that men and women are fundamentally different often have difficulty making the differences clear. Because both men and women are made in the image of God, we share many aspects of our being; also, masculinity and femininity are often seen in degrees of intensity or emphasis in traits that are found in both sexes.

However, Adam's creation as leader and provider would cause us to expect men to more naturally display character traits that aid in those responsibilities, such as aggressiveness, initiative, logical analysis, objectivity, perseverance. We would expect men's attention to be focused more on accomplishment and control, on performance and success.

Eve's creation as helper and companion, on the other hand, would cause us to expect women to more naturally display traits that would aid them in those responsibilities: gentleness, responsiveness, emotional perception, encouragement, cooperation. We would expect women's attention to be turned more toward relationship and harmony, advocacy and nurture.

Let me give a caveat here: Women may exercise many vocations that include leadership (mothers, employers, teachers, etc.); men may exercise many vocations that require submission to others' leadership (sons, employees, students, etc.). Right now I wish to establish the vocation of sex as I see it at creation and specifically relating to the family, established by God as the first social unit. How the vocation of sex plays itself out when the specific responsibilities I am discussing here are "reversed" I will discuss a little further on.

What does it mean to lead? How do we describe the vocation of leadership? Since we are looking at family relationships, a reminder of the purpose of the family might help. Adam and Eve were given the task of subduing the earth. As husband and wife, they were to cleave to one another. The New Testament furthers our understanding of the "one flesh" mystery: Marriage is to be a picture of the relationship between Christ and the church. From these we could perhaps create a basic mission statement for the family: "To glorify God and edify our neighbors by good stewardship of God's creation and by demonstrating the relationship God wishes to have with His children through Jesus Christ."

The one who leads this family—the husband and father—holds the ultimate responsibility for the fulfillment of this mission. He represents the family to others, protects it from outside threats and inner dissension, decides what tasks are needed to fulfill its mission, and delegates certain of those tasks while remaining responsible for their successful fulfillment. He will be the one who sees the "big picture" and leads his family toward its fulfillment. His vision will tend to be focused on this achievement.

The wife and mother's vocation is to be her husband's helpmeet. She will strive to understand and embrace the family's mission, to accept the responsibilities delegated to her, and to do her best to accomplish them excellently so that the family may succeed in its mission. She will recognize the responsibility given to her husband and will willingly submit to his authority so he can give a good account to the One who placed him as the leader.

A woman's focus, then, is more likely to be on the particular tasks she is given than on the whole, on the welfare of the people she works with and for rather than on the purpose of the tasks. While her husband may sometimes need to remind her of the family's ultimate mission as the reason for some difficult step that must be taken, she may sometimes need to remind him that within that mission are individuals who need to be attended to as emotional beings, not merely cogs in a machine.

I'm reminded of a conversation at our faculty lunch table recently, when the father of a new baby remarked that he'd had no difficulty forcing medicine into the infant despite his screaming and fighting because the ultimate goal of the child's health was more important than his immediate comfort. His wife, fully understanding the need, struggled more in persevering to accomplish the task, because the child's immediate turmoil devastated her mother's heart; she was in tears while her husband was quite matter-of-fact.

There may come a time later, however, when this father's focus on a goal will threaten to harm the legitimate emotional needs of this child. Perhaps he will be so intent on training the child to use some special ability as part of the family's public ministry, for example, that he will overlook a natural reticence and consequent fearfulness that needs to be taken into account and dealt with gently. Here his wife's emotional connection to the child can help her husband find a more gradual, more compassionate way of achieving the goal than the demand for immediate performance.

This is the pattern I believe God intended in creating man and woman—two equal but different beings, meant to complement each other in a creative partnership that will glorify Him. The differences He built in are not differences in kind so much as emphasis. A woman's compassion, for example, should balance a man's logic, but also remind him of his need to develop and show compassion, even if it is somewhat less natural to him to do so.

"We are called to exemplify all the virtues," Ronda Chervin, philosophy professor at Our Lady of Corpus Christi College, reminds us in discussing what she calls "quality-complementarity" (50). Though a woman more naturally practices feminine traits such as tenderness and sensitivity, if she does not balance these with a mature development of traits such as strength and objectivity, which are more naturally masculine, she will likely be overly passive, manipulative, irresponsible, silly. On the other hand, if she focuses on developing masculine traits while repressing her natural feminine ones, she will be domineering, harsh, aggressive, demanding. Neither extreme is truly feminine.

The same principle applies to men, of course. Men who focus on developing solely masculine traits may become "at worst, tyrannical and brutal, and, at best, patronizing, paternalistic and smug" (Chervin, 51). And a man who develops feminine traits while repressing his natural masculine ones will be effeminate and ineffective.

This concept explains both the passive, victim-oriented woman Van Leeuwen describes and the domineering, cold woman we see more and more often in business and academia today. It explains the harsh, tyrannical husband and the one who refuses to take leadership at all. But the balanced personality is not androgynous. Balanced women are always identifiably women, and balanced men are always identifiably men.

Let's explore the concept in parenting, for example. Children tend to run to mothers first for comfort and affection, to fathers first for action. And when it comes to obedience and discipline, Dad's voice is usually obeyed quickest. Almost any child would prefer to face Mom with the rod rather than Dad, even in families where Mom is a consistent disciplinarian and Dad a compassionate one. Why is this?

A mother is naturally tenderhearted toward her children. She doesn't wish to see them hurt; she would like to smooth their path as much as possible. She is quick to offer comfort, to give hugs, to praise and encourage. It is natural for her children to respond to this aspect of her nature with their affection.

However, a mother's temptation is to be lax in discipline or overly helpful in rough times. To avoid this, she must develop her less-strong abilities in order to see objectively and to be strong in holding to principles. She shows her tenderness in her words, her expression, but doesn't back down. By doing so, her firmness proves that her tenderness is genuine love, and she earns her children's respect along with their affection.

A father, on the other hand, more naturally reacts with objectivity and strength of principle in all his dealings with his children. They may have lots of fun together, but he won't smooth the path, and they soon learn that minor hurts of any sort are to be brushed off quickly. His children respond naturally to these traits with respect.

A father's temptation, however, is to be cold or harsh in training and disciplining his children. He must develop his less-strong abilities to empathize and to comfort, so that the sting of honest assessment ("you didn't do that well; do it over") or needed discipline won't turn into resentment. In doing so, his tenderness proves that his strength is genuine love, and he earns his children's affection along with their respect.

In both cases, natural feminine and masculine traits are balanced—but not negated or overpowered—by the development of complementary traits. Each parent retains his or her natural character as dominant but is capable of acting in complementary ways when necessary.

I find the example of parenting easiest to develop in explaining quality-complementarity, though we will see it at work elsewhere as well. This is partly because marriage is the most obvious and intimate male-female relationship, I suppose, and our complementary traits are most clearly seen in how we relate to our children. However, it is also because I believe that not only the woman's creation as helpmeet and companion causes her to have the feminine traits we have been discussing, but as much or even more so her ability to bear and nourish children. Carrying a life within one's own body, nourishing a helpless, completely dependent infant at the breast, caring for his every physical and emotional need—any woman who does not understand at least to some extent the beauty of giving herself entirely to another in this way is repressing something natural within her soul. And any man who is not awed by this potential and moved to protect and provide for the mother of his children does not understand true manhood; he denies his own God-given being.

This is why abortion appalls and horrifies me. While I empathize with women who find themselves in a desperate situation, I am horrified that our culture has so denied natural womanhood and manhood that we seem to truly believe that the murder of innocent children is an acceptable alternative to chastity or, failing that, adoption. The madness of radical feminism is clearest to me in this issue: women demanding the right to destroy lives that were meant to bring out the best of their womanhood.

And when I think of the millions of women who have been deceived by this lie, only to find that their souls finally rebel by leaving them guilty and depressed, my heart breaks. Where are the feminists when the women they deceive face the consequences of their lies? It is not the feminists who open their hearts to grieving mothers, who provide counseling, who try to show them the way to forgiveness. Sadly, it is far too often not the church either. Women betrayed by other women, by this self-centered, hedonistic culture, by men who don't understand true manhood—these women need the healing power of God's forgiveness, and it must begin with our acceptance of them and reaching out to them to let God show them His love through us.

I am not suggesting that women must bear children to be fully women. Obviously there are women, single and married, who go through life without children, yet are just as fully women as any mother. But I do believe this *potential* to bear children is at least part of what causes us to have the natural character traits that we do. Woman was created to be a helpmeet, a companion, and a *nurturer*. If she doesn't have children to nurture, she will still nurture other people (and mothers nurture others besides their children). Watch any little girl with her dolls or with a younger sibling. As she grows, watch how she interacts with her friends. This is the call of womanhood: "to live out our love for others day by day in faithfulness" (Chervin, 63).

I have been exploring manhood and womanhood in the direct context of creation and the family. God created Adam to lead and Eve to be his helpmeet, and He gave each the primary character traits that are most beneficial to those roles. However, again, women often exercise vocations of leadership, while men find themselves in vocations that require submission to others, including at times women. How does this fit with what we have just discussed concerning the vocation of sex itself? If men are created to lead and women to be helpmeets, and if the character traits we see in each seem to correlate with these "roles," then how can women lead and men follow without violating these created distinctions?

First of all, remember that vocation has to do with our relationships to others. While it is true that I am always a woman— and that, I believe, always affects my attitude and actions—every relation I have with others is not *primarily based* on my womanhood. I owe the dean of my college submission because he is my employer, not because he is a man and I am a woman. (I would owe the same submission to a female dean, as would my male colleagues.) As an employee, I am no different in my relationship to my dean than any of the male faculty who teach alongside me. I may tend to express both my compliance and my concerns in a different manner from my male colleagues, because I am female, but my words are not valued because I am a woman; they are valued because I am an employee.

In the same way, the students in my classroom are to submit to my authority because I am the teacher; my sex is beside the point, as is theirs. The vocation of teacher requires that I make certain demands of them, just as the vocation of student requires that those in my classroom comply with those demands, regardless of the sex of any of us. I am in charge in my classroom, and my students know it. Compassion doesn't override my marking an F for incomplete or incompetent work, any more than it keeps me from giving appropriate discipline to one of my children. My desire to encourage and nurture my students doesn't keep me from giving an objective assessment of their performance or from insisting that they follow classroom decorum and the rules laid down in the syllabus. These are simply the duties of any teacher, and I carry them out without regard to the sex of any individual student.

Yet I have seen some differences in the ways my male colleagues and I approach our tasks that are rooted, I believe, in the traits we naturally emphasize because of the vocation of sex. As a rule, my male colleagues tend to find unpleasant conversations about grades somewhat easier than I do. Not that they necessarily lack compassion for students who are upset—they just seem better able to remain focused on the facts of the situation while I struggle more to maintain an appearance of steadfast toughness as I *feel* the frustration of the student facing me. On the other hand, I've known students who found it easier to accept a poor grade from me as they encountered more obvious empathy and encouragement than they sometimes find from their male professors. These are ways we can help each other learn to acquire a balance of "feminine" and "masculine" traits in our interactions with students, similar, even in such a less intimate environment, to the way husbands and wives complement each other and help each other toward balance.

The issue of manhood and womanhood, then, does not always have to do with the roles of leadership and submission. The vocation of sex gives us certain character qualities as our strengths, others that we must develop as a balance, and these are rooted in the creation of family roles. It does not, however, necessarily constrain us to certain roles in areas outside of family and church leadership. Who leads and who follows is generally a matter of who is qualified to do so, regardless of sex. Yet the character traits of our vocation of sex will generally affect the ways we carry out our roles, even when the results of our performance are identical.

I am not, however, convinced that because women can appropriately hold leadership roles they ought to do *anything* that men do in the society at large. While I do not see any scriptural basis for denying women many positions of authority and many career options that have not always been open to us, yet I believe that the differences of the sexes, innate from Creation, limit appropriate roles for women to some degree even outside of family and church leadership.

For one thing, mere physical differences ensure that women will never be able to perform certain tasks as efficiently as men. A recent *20/20 Downtown* documentary on women in the military highlighted (though perhaps not intentionally) the absurdity of women as combat soldiers (Raphael). Even the best-conditioned cannot do many of the tasks required of soldiers, creating a divisive atmosphere instead of camaraderie as the men are forced to take on extra burdens. Our military effectiveness is being seriously compromised by placing women in combat positions. Physical standards are being lowered so they can succeed, and sexual liaisons place a burden on all members of a unit. Also, men, because of their natural desire to protect women, must be trained out of that desire or risk placing a woman's safety above the achievement of a unit's goal. These are not small issues; they leave our entire nation vulnerable if our military cannot effectively protect us. (See Webb, Aspy.)

Other careers present the same problem. Personally I am not interested in the appearance of a female law enforcement officer as the first on the scene if my safety is being threatened by a man; she may well not have the physical ability to do her duty of protecting me. A female firefighter cannot carry as much length of hose as a man, nor can she pull a large person from a burning building by herself. In all these areas, women may have a place to serve—but not where physical strength may make the difference between safety and harm.

Some other professions may not be wise for women to pursue. While I have no problem with women enjoying sports, I have been concerned with the pressure to make women's sports in college as intense as men's, and the advent of more and more professional women's sports. According to some, when women train too hard and too long, as many college and professional athletes must to succeed, their reproductive systems are placed under stress that we do not yet know the seriousness of. Will some of these women find that their pursuit of athletic success has robbed them of what they may realize too late is far more important in the long run—children to love and nurture? In any case, a woman should realistically consider her abilities and her

long-term goals before deciding to pursue a career or activity
that may have been traditionally male for good reason.

To be a woman in every relationship we have is the call of
love. This is so, Luther tells us, because "it is by God's own
ordering that the work of the [vocation] is always dedicated to
the well-being of one's neighbor" (Wingren, 9). But this dedica-
tion does not come without cost; it is vocation that forces us to
discipline ourselves and die daily to the old self. It is in being
compelled to be concerned with other people that we become
helpless before God and there is opportunity for faith to be born.
Every vocation involves trials and difficulties—a cross—that we
are to bear for the benefit of our neighbors; only when I die to
myself am I able to do good to others. Simple daily life will bring
us the suffering promised in Scripture to the Christian. This suffering, however, is exactly what pushes us toward faith, as we
see that we cannot in ourselves bear all the responsibilities of our
various vocations. In fact, "as soon as vocation is abandoned,
God loses hold of man, faith and love cease, and . . . the devil
. . . has gained control of man" (Wingren, 33).

Luther uses the analogy of nature to point out a principle of
vocation: As nature bestows its gifts on people regardless of their
merit (the rain falls "on the just and the unjust," Matt. 5:45), so
Christian love "must be willing to be misused, and to be a 'lost
love'" (Wingren, 171). In other words, as we love our neighbors
through our vocation, they will not necessarily be appreciative
or respond positively to us or to God. This, Luther says, causes
a great temptation to the believer to be discontent with his vocation, to wish for some work that will gain him more recognition.
"He is tempted to do something other than his vocation, something that has more meaning and receives some measure of
recognition from the world. But the conflict between God and
the devil demands that God's work have appearances against it

in a world deranged by sin; and all false byways have appearances in their favor. This must involve an inner struggle for one who is employed in his vocation. He often stands alone with the day's task, without guidance from God's people, with God's command as his only support and prayer as his only resource" (Wingren, 171).

This, I believe, is a major reason for much feminist discourse, including that which we are hearing in the church. In a society as individualistic and achievement-oriented as ours, the role of nurturer and helper is not valued or recognized. The one who works behind the scenes is not the one whose name is in lights on the marquee, and our culture values only the name on the marquee, suggesting that any of us can achieve fame and prosperity if we try hard enough, and that this indeed should be our aim. Thus, a woman's more natural concerns for relationship and family are seen as weak and her traditional role—or any role not leading to public recognition and high status—as menial and demeaning, unworthy of anyone with intelligence. However, God sees things differently.

The One who created us as women knows what our needs and our failings are. He recognizes the very real problems that women face in any society, problems brought about by sin in its many guises, and He cares that those problems be solved. Our biggest mistake, always, is looking to the culture or to our mere human reason for solutions when His Word alone lights the path.

God created Adam to lovingly lead and Eve to willingly respond. They were intended to work together as partners at the tasks given—to tend the Garden and have dominion over the earth, filling it with more of their kind. The Fall itself was precipitated by the reversal of those roles, Eve choosing to deny her vocation as a woman and to encourage Adam to disobey God's clear command, Adam choosing to deny his vocation as a man and to willingly follow her lead. The curse they brought upon themselves through their denial of the natures God had given them is the root of all our troubles since, leaving us with sin natures that manifest themselves in every conceivable way, including in the ways we relate to each other as men and women, competing and quarreling instead of working together joyfully in creative partnership.

But God, in his unfathomable love for us fallen creatures, sent His Son to redeem us from the curse of the Fall. His grace offers us the hope of breaking the sinful patterns of domination and desire for control and of living together more nearly as He originally intended. We can only do this, however, if we understand that gender itself is a vocation, that men and women were created differently, and that our differences show us the way to harmonious relationships. As biology professor Gregg Johnson, concluding a review of the biological differences between men and women, says, "Let us hope that, by recognizing the existence of gender differences, we can better understand each other and help to maximize each other's potentials. Likewise, by accepting our God-given gifts, we can resist cultural pressures to become what we are not and to seek to master gifts we don't possess" (293).

God gives women differing gifts and places us within a variety of circumstances. It is His intention that we be fulfilled through our gifts and in our circumstances, yet always within the parameters of our first gift and circumstance: our womanhood. It is in our return to this most basic vocation—the call to be a woman—that we will find contentment and begin to see how we can answer the questions facing us as Christian women in a fallen world. However, as we are reminded by Luther, "The sign of a right ethic is not found in a certain fixed outward behavior, but in the ability to meet, in calmness and faith, whatever may come" (Wingren, 181). Therefore, as I explore what it means to be a woman in some of our most important relationships, my goal is not to prescribe roles—except where prescribed in Scripture—but to look at some of the principles God gives that can guide us to the specific answers He has for each of us. While I obviously can't address all issues or make all applications, I hope to suggest at least a broad sense of what it means to be particularly a woman in this journey through life—and to celebrate the freedom and joy that womanhood offers.

CHAPTER SIX

The Battle of the Sexes

ᔕ

"Women—can't live with 'em, can't live without 'em."
"Isn't that just like a man?"

The battle between the sexes has raged since Adam cast the blame on Eve for his sin in the Garden. God, of course, didn't create us to be adversaries but companions and complements. Then the Fall left us with sin natures, parts of which include man's tendency to lord power over the women in his life and woman's tendency to desire inappropriate control and independence. Redemption in Christ frees us from the power of sin, but fleshly patterns and worldly influences can confuse our daily walk and our understanding of the masculine and feminine natures God has given us.

Marriage, of course, is the closest relationship between a man and a woman—and the one most damaged by the Fall. As this is a book about women, I am concentrating primarily on what womanhood is about. However, far too often much is made of a woman's role of submission without clarifying what a man's role of leadership is all about; therefore, although we looked at this issue in Chapter 5, I wish to review it briefly here.

I have shown why I believe that God intended Adam for loving leadership and Eve for his helpmeet. But what is loving leadership? Obviously God did not create Eve to be a slave to Adam's every whim! Created from Adam's very body, she is his equal in intelligence and talent and discernment and is to be valued for her ideas and abilities, her uniquely feminine personhood. Adam rejoices over her because he has found a companion suitable for him in every way, his complement.

The New Testament clearly tells us how a Christian husband is to lead in his home—and it has nothing to do with controlling his wife or ordering her around or treating her as a lesser being who should have no opinions except the ones he gives her. In Ibsen's *A Doll House* Torvald treats Nora as a child, dictating her every move and thought, causing her in turn to become secretive and deceptive. God's way is far different. He calls husbands to love their wives "as Christ . . . loved the church and gave Himself for her." They are to love their wives "as their own bodies; he who loves his wife loves himself." The Christian husband "nourishes and cherishes" his wife as Christ does the church (Eph. 5:25-29). Husbands are not to be "bitter" toward their wives (Col. 3:19). They are to live with their wives with "understanding, giving honor" to them (1 Pet. 3:7).

Dr. Nicholas A. Beadles II, associate professor of management at Georgia College and State University, describes biblically based leadership as a form of stewardship. A steward, Beadles notes, is "one entrusted by God with spiritual authority and responsibility and is thus responsible to God for how he discharges those duties." In application to the family, a man who leads his wife is God's steward of her, responsible not so much to her as to God for her welfare. He is the servant of Christ who, in submitting to his Savior, cares for those under his authority in the same way Christ cares for His church.

Sadly, far too many Christians, men and women alike, do not understand this loving leadership that men are to exercise. If a man finds himself saying, "You don't respect my authority," he has a problem—he is more concerned with power than with responsibility. The ideal Christian husband will lay down his life to see his wife content, using her talents and gifts in the way God intends, living her life in a joyful response to God first, then to him. He will not be concerned with the issue of her submission because his cherishing of her will draw her to desire his leadership; he will not be inclined to lord it over her because he is focused on loving her.

Of course, though I do know a good many who are trying to be, no man is ideal. We women have to deal with the imperfect men who are our husbands, and God has given us clear instruction on how to do so. That instruction will only be effective when we acknowledge our own sinful tendency to desire control and the ways we go about trying to get it. Once we understand this, along with God's intentions in creating woman as man's helpmeet, we can understand the New Testament commands to wives.

"Wives, submit to your own husbands, as to the Lord . . . just as the church is subject to Christ, so let wives be to their own husbands in everything . . . let the wife see that she respects her husband" (Eph. 5:22, 24, 33). "Wives, submit to your own husbands, as is fitting in the Lord" (Col. 3:18). "Wives, likewise be submissive to your own husbands, that even if some do not obey the word, they, without a word, may be won by the conduct of their wives, when they observe your chaste conduct accompanied by fear" (1 Pet. 3:1-2).

The Greek word translated *submission* or *subjection* in these verses is *hupotasso*, which, according to *Strong's Concordance*, is "a Greek military term meaning 'to arrange [troop divisions] in a military fashion under the command of a leader.' In non-military use, it was 'a voluntary attitude of giving in, cooperating, assuming responsibility, and carrying a burden.'" The word is used numerous times in the New Testament, applying to such varying circumstances as Jesus' submission to His parents (Luke 2:51), submission to the righteousness of God (Rom. 10:3), the ultimate subjection of all things to Christ (1 Cor. 15:27), the submission of servants to their masters (Titus 2:9; 1 Pet. 2:18), and our submission to government (1 Pet. 2:13).

To place the concept in a different, less volatile context than marriage, consider the dean of a college. He could be somewhere else, doing a different job, but chooses to remain under the authority of the president of the college. He is not a lesser person in any sense of the word. His counsel is sought after regularly and is valued and often taken; many decisions are made jointly and agreed on by both. He often initiates new ideas, many of which will be implemented. But the president has the authority—and the responsibility—to make final decisions; and the dean will, if he values the president and the college, voluntarily agree to abide by those decisions and to do what is required of him to make them successful. He will also have many areas of authority delegated to him for his sole responsibility. Remembering that it is his employer who is ultimately accountable for the success or failure of the college, he will prove himself a trustworthy worker, putting the college's welfare ahead of personal concerns.

The covenant of marriage binds husband and wife far more closely and permanently than a worldly contract, of course. But the analogy holds in certain of the ways a husband and wife relate to one another. A wife is clearly not a slave or a doormat. Her submission to her husband is voluntary; she is a cooperative partner in the marriage who has particular responsibilities and burdens that she bears so that he is free to give his full attention to other responsibilities. She works *with* him for the good of the marriage and family. The wife is just as valued and necessary as the husband, but the husband has been given ultimate responsibility for the family's welfare. The wife who respects this responsibility will not demand her own way, for if the husband gives in to her and she is wrong, he is still held responsible, just as Adam was held responsible for the decision made in the Garden. Remember that God called on Adam first after the Fall, not Eve, even though she was the first to sin. It is also through Adam that the sin nature is passed on (Rom. 5:12: "Therefore, just as through one man sin entered the world, and death through sin . . .").

So submission does not mean a wife is a doormat. She is an equal and equally valued contributor to the success of the family. Her husband discusses decisions with her, listens to her ideas and concerns, values her contributions. She is in charge of many aspects of family life, and he trusts her to carry out her tasks effectively: "The heart of her husband safely trusts her; so he will have no lack of gain. She does him good and not evil all the days of her life" (Prov. 31:11-12). But because even godly Christian men are not perfect, there may be times when she has to decide how to respond to a decision her husband makes that she believes is wrong. If the husband's decision is sinful, her response is clear: to appeal to him on the basis of Scripture to change his mind, and if he doesn't, refuse to join him in the sinful action, yet with a respectful attitude. However, if the decision is not a clearly sinful one, her response will be more difficult. She should, of course, express her opinion and try to persuade him to see her view. But ultimately, if she places her trust in God rather than man, she will accept the decision and let God deal with her husband's heart.

I know a couple who had a disagreement over seat belts for their children when they were too small to strap themselves in. (This was back in the dark ages before car seat and seat belt laws!) The wife protested that the children were unsafe without wearing seat belts; the husband shrugged off her protest because it was a hassle to get into the backseat of the vehicle and strap the kids in. The wife went to the Lord, who reminded her to submit, and finally accepted the husband's decision graciously, though with much prayer for the safety of the two boys. A few days after she stopped her worrisome nagging, her husband had to make a sudden stop, and a child came tumbling into the front seat, screaming in terror. He was unhurt, but suddenly it was no longer a hassle for his father to make sure the youngster and his brother were safely strapped in.

A small example, but one that impressed on this woman the need to stop arguing after having made her point and to let God deal with her husband when he chose not to listen to her. Of course, there may be times when issues are not as clear-cut, and different women have convictions that would lead them to act differently. I think of Corrie ten Boom's and her sister's differing convictions about lying to protect the Jews they were hiding in their house. But God honored each sister's conviction when each was called on to decide how to respond to a direct question about their activities. Corrie believed that it was appropriate to lie when the questioner's motive was to harm innocent people; when she falsely told the SS officers there were no Jews in their home, they were left alone. Her sister, on the other hand, believed that any lie for any reason was sin, but when she directly told an SS patrol that Jews were indeed hiding in their home, they missed the trap door beneath the table and left frustrated. I believe God honored both because each was convinced before the Lord that her interpretation of Scripture was right on this point; furthermore, each loved God and desired only to serve Him righteously. Of course, if those (hopefully rare) occasions of conflict occur, the fellowship and counsel of other godly women is important for wives.

But what about the woman whose marriage is definitely in trouble because of a husband's lack of godliness? I know of a woman ensnared in adultery whose mistakes others could profit from. First, she aired complaints about her husband to another man—not seeking counsel, but seeking an avenue for her understandable frustration. Next, she listened when that man sympathized with her by sharing about his problems with his wife. Then she convinced herself that they were "counseling" each other, when in reality he was setting the stage to seduce her, which she later discovered was a pattern in his life. Now, this woman's problems were real, her husband didn't believe he was contributing to them, and she needed counsel. She could, however, have avoided the affair that occurred by taking certain precautions.

First, she was more concerned with finding sympathy than with finding solutions. She needed to realize she couldn't change her husband, only herself, and to start seeking what she could actively do to make the marriage better; it's extremely rare in a difficult marriage that only one partner holds the entire blame. Instead of discussing her problems with another man because he seemed sympathetic to her, she should have sought out a godly older woman and/or a professional Christian counselor who would have held her accountable for her own actions and helped her see how she could begin to mend the marriage, instead of feeding her sense of victimization and self-righteousness. Only by taking responsibility for herself could she have accomplished the goal she claimed to seek—reconciliation. Because she never did this, her marriage finally ended, utterly destroyed.

The story contains a warning for all of us married women. While we must feel free to seek counsel for genuine problems, we must also have enough respect for our husbands and our marriages to exercise caution in how and to whom we speak about them. God hates divorce, and Christ died not only for our reconciliation to God, but also so we would have the power to be reconciled to each other. The more we speak to others about problems we have, the more we magnify those problems; then the less respect we generate for either ourselves or our spouse, and the harder it is to bring about the reconciliation God desires. We must put our marriages above our mere feelings of sadness or anger. And we must be willing to recognize our own sinful responses and actions, being willing to make changes in ourselves to bring about change in our marriage.

Concerning male authority, the single woman is in a different position from her married sister. If she lives at home, she is at least under some obligation to her father, though as an adult she is directly responsible to God for her choices. This becomes a difficult area for my college students, who are often being partially or completely supported by their parents. They do not always find God's call on their lives to be the same as their parents' wishes, and how do they juggle these? I have spent many an hour helping young women try to find this line, and it is not always in the same place. Usually the spiritual maturity of the young woman defines my advice: Does she really desire to follow God, or is she just trying to get out of responsibility to her parents?

One dear friend tells how her decidedly unsaved father refused to agree to her engagement to a young Christian man. Deciding to take his refusal as being from the Lord was a painful experience. Yet later that young man turned out to be very spiritually weak, and she realized she had been spared a life filled with pain. Her father approved of another Christian man who wanted to marry her ("I can't find anything wrong with him except that he's a Christian," he told her), and she has had a wonderfully happy journey as a pastor's wife. Not all parents, believers or unbelievers, will be as discerning as this father; yet any single woman should prayerfully consider her parents' counsel, even if she is living away from home and supporting herself entirely. They do, after all, know her well and can offer her knowledge and wisdom beyond her years. Luther tells us vocation governs the relationships of all people, not just believers. Unbelieving parents are still parents, and children are still to honor them, so that "it may be well with [them] and [they] may live long on the earth" (Eph. 6:3).

Women have many different relationships with men. It is important to consider the context of each relationship to know if we are acting appropriately. All believers, of course, are to respect the authority of an employer and of civil authorities. In these relationships, even though the authority is not based on the male/female dynamic, a woman still can respond *as a woman*— with "a gentle and quiet spirit" that respects the men she encounters *as men*, acknowledging the character traits God has given them.

An area that can be touchy is the circumstance in which a woman is in a position of authority over men. How can she exercise that authority without acting like a man or without offending the men under her supervision? Vocation, of course, is the key, as we discussed in Chapter 5. A woman who leads, say as an employer or administrator, does the same things as a man who leads: She is responsible to articulate the mission of her group and see that it is carried out, to delegate tasks to that end, to represent the group to others, to protect the group as necessary from external and internal threats. To do this well, she will certainly need to have developed character traits such as logical analysis, objectivity, perseverance, etc., traits that we more commonly associate with men than with women, but, as we have seen, should be developed to some degree by everyone.

One challenge for a woman in leadership is to develop these traits without letting them completely override her feminine traits, becoming "like a man" in order to gain the respect of the men in her field, including (perhaps especially?) those under her authority. I see this as a similar issue to parenting; my children can know that I am in charge without my being just like their dad. A woman employer or administrator can gain respect by her competence and firmness without giving up her natural bent to encourage and nurture those she leads.

In leading in this way, a woman provides an example to her male colleagues of leadership that does not have to be totally controlling or cold in its honesty. This is one reason I believe having women in the workforce in leadership positions is beneficial to a culture. If, however, women leaders merely act in the same ways as male leaders who have refused to develop some of their more feminine traits, they are throwing away an opportunity to do far more than experience mere personal success.

A woman on an administration team made up of mostly men can also offer perspectives that might otherwise be overlooked. Male administrators in one college where I taught were in the habit of handing down decisions in a brusque, matter-of-fact way that often elicited a negative response from employees who were affected by those decisions. A woman on the team helped them to see the consequences of their typically male style of communication and to find ways of wording their memos and reports that took into account the emotional responses of their audience. She also encouraged them to more genuinely listen to the concerns of employees, even when a decision was inevitable, in an effort to address those concerns in creative ways rather than dismissing them as impossible. Her presence began to give the team a balance it had been sorely lacking, to the benefit of the entire college. She was, by the way, able to express her opinions with the same decisiveness and tenacity as any man on the team; her wording was gracious but her messages unmistakable as she worked for balance in her own personality as well as in the group of which she was a part.

By retaining femininity in exercising authority, women can bring to the workplace a sense of compassion and encouragement, of gentleness in dealings with others. Often women are the ones quick to notice others' moods, to leave notes of encouragement or congratulations, to pay attention to birthdays and births, to create a pleasing physical environment. However, in acting in these ways, a woman must also be cautious not to imply availability for inappropriate relationships. We must remember that the various vocations we exercise are not separate compartments of our lives. I do not cease to be a wife when I enter my office at the college; my relationships to my male colleagues are governed not solely by our common vocation of teaching but also by the vocation of marriage, which does not allow for flirtatiousness or meetings behind closed doors.

I think, for example, of the incident that occurred during Gary Bauer's aborted bid for the presidency. I believe there was no improper relationship between him and the single young woman who was part of his campaign; yet his meeting long hours with her behind closed doors should never have happened. To me, this incident showed just how insidiously and completely the world's philosophy continues to work its way into our thinking despite our relationship with Christ. Bauer, as a married Christian man and older adult, certainly was the one primarily responsible for allowing the situation to occur at all, especially after the concern shown by staff members. Yet the young woman herself could have insisted on open doors and the participation of others in at least many of their conversations.

The world says, "How silly this concern is!" Of course, the world believes adultery is nothing to be concerned over either, and yet God tells us to flee temptation, that even entertaining lustful thoughts is a sin. So how much more is it sinful to allow situations to occur in which we might act on such desires. Remember the young woman I mentioned earlier who became ensnared in adultery merely because she began sharing some of her marital problems with a seemingly sympathetic man who then offered to "counsel" her—privately. Had she simply refused to meet with him behind closed doors in the first place, the entire affair would never have happened.

These incidents bring up an important and, I believe, fundamental virtue we can practice to honor both our womanhood and the manhood of the men in our lives: modesty. Modesty is often mocked today and seems almost lost in our contemporary culture, including within the church. Yet, although both men in the instances above bear primary responsibility for their actions, if the two women had understood the virtue of modesty, neither would have placed herself in a position to invite speculation or adultery.

Wendy Shalit's *A Return to Modesty* is a compelling—and chilling—look at the results of the radical feminists' pursuit of equality in the arena of sexual relationships. In their attempts to erase or deny all natural differences between the sexes, the feminists have proclaimed that sexuality means nothing more to women than to men, thereby destroying the one thing that Shalit claims gave women genuine protection against abuse of various sorts—female modesty.

Shalit chronicles the increasing problems women face today,

from sexual harassment to rape, from eating disorders to suicide. She then points out that such problems were far less common before our attempts to create an "egalitarian" society. Women in the nineteenth century, according to de Tocqueville's observations of the American scene, could walk anywhere they pleased, with or without an escort, simply because men respected all women as "ladies." Now we're told that this is a "sexist" idea, and women are treated like public property by every boor that passes by. "Maybe treating all women respectfully was not subordinating, after all," Shalit says, "but precisely a way of conveying that they were not mere property" (46).

Lest anyone think I am advocating a return to high-necked, long-sleeved dresses that reach the floor, let me affirm that modesty is relative to one's culture and has to do with attitude as much as external appearance. We have all seen women dressed in clothing that mostly covers them who nonetheless give out clear signals of an inappropriate availability. And when Peter addresses clothing, it is secondary to the heart: We shouldn't adorn ourselves with flashy clothes and hairstyles, but instead "let it be the hidden person of the heart, with the incorruptible beauty of a gentle and quiet spirit, which is very precious in the sight of God" (1 Pet. 3:4).

Shalit defines modesty as "a reflex, arising naturally to help a woman protect her hopes and guide their fulfillment—specifically, this hope for one man" (94). She makes an excellent case for the naturalness of women's desire for home, family, commitment. Men, she says, can be won to commitment only when their desire for irresponsible sexual fulfillment is thwarted by most of the women in a society; when women don't readily give away sexual favors, men will behave honorably toward them and consider them as worthy marriage partners.

I clearly recall a disturbing conversation in the writing center of one of the Christian colleges where I've taught. Both male and female students were present, and somehow the talk turned to matters of femininity and sexuality that I had always considered private. Two or three women might discuss such matters together, but never a mixed group. I was appalled at the casualness of all the students, especially the women, and I pretty quickly retired to my office, remarking, "I guess I'm too old-fashioned for this."

Later I discussed the occurrence with one of the students. This particular young woman dressed modestly at all times, had not started dating until she met a young man she thought she might marry, and was completely committed to premarital chastity, being very cautious in her physical contact with her boyfriend. Yet she seemed quite at ease with conversation that I—a forty-four-year-old married woman with children—was thoroughly embarrassed by. She conceded that the conversation was less than modest but told me, in essence, "We're all used to it; we've been talking about this stuff in coed classes for years."

I had thought Shalit's claim that not having participated in sex education classes had set her apart from her peers might have been rather simplistic. Now I wonder. The young woman I talked to was unusual in her convictions; sexual activity on that primarily Christian-professing campus was common. I knew that surveys of Christian colleges across the U.S. had shown that an alarmingly high number of young men expected sexual favors from their dates. Although a significantly lower number of girls agreed with them in the surveys, apparently far too many gave in to those expectations anyway. And where better to start such a trend than in coed sex education classes, where natural shame and embarrassment are purposefully broken down to make us "comfortable with our bodies," as the mantra goes.

I am profoundly saddened that our Christian young women

have so little respect for themselves and for the men they encounter. I am appalled that the church has apparently done such a poor job in convincing them that the secular teaching they have received is all wrong. I would like to join Wendy Shalit in a call for women to embrace their hopes and not be afraid to challenge a culture that would rob them of their most precious dreams.

That challenge begins, of course, with an inner decision that as a woman I will maintain my self-respect and believe that I am worthy of the respect of others—and that no man who wants merely to use me for physical pleasure, without the commitment of marriage, is worthy of my commitment to him. As Shalit says, if enough women would decide this, men would *have* to start acting respectfully toward us again! But even if others don't, however lonely it may at times seem, a woman who honors God with her commitment to purity will not be abandoned by Him. And a man who is worthy is well worth waiting for; the heartaches of women who settle for less are far worse than even a lifetime of loneliness.

I am not, by the way, saying to look at men as monsters! As Shalit says, the men of her generation are products of the culture also. A couple of generations ago men acted respectfully toward women as a rule, because it was expected and there were social consequences to pay if they did not. Today's young men are mostly merely ignorant. They have been told that women are no different from men, that casual sex is a normal way of life; they have never been taught that women value decency and respect. If we can understand this, we can use our own return to modesty to educate men and help them desire to become honorable in their dealings with women.

How does this commitment work itself out in practical ways? As I've mentioned, modesty is relative to culture; there are cultures where nudity or near-nudity is the norm, yet there are still conventions of modesty, things women do and don't do, actions they accept from men and refuse to accept. But in our western culture, dress does play an important part in modesty; and far too many young women, and even women in my generation, have no idea what constitutes modest dress.

I recall wondering how the mothers in a church I once attended could let their daughters wear skirts that came more than halfway up their thighs—until I saw how the mothers were dressed. Why do we seem to think that we can dress any way we please and expect men to keep their eyes (and their hands) to themselves? This seems to me basic physiology. Men are easily aroused by sight; so women, if they honor men, should seek to dress in such a way that overtly sexual attention is not drawn to their bodies. Yet we need to teach our young women this. I see some of the most immodest dress on students who I am sure are not consciously trying to attract men inappropriately—they just haven't been taught what messages their clothing sends.

Shalit quotes Muslim women who are quite content with the "oppressive" (according to their feminist sisters) hejab—the robe and veil that conceals all but the eyes. One such woman remarks, "In order to prevent our natural feelings for the opposite sex from overpowering our logic and dictating our behavior, it is prescribed that in public both men and women should cover themselves up" (quoted on 218). Another says, "Veiled women are much more attractive than unveiled women. . . . One of the reasons sex died in the West was because they have no veils" (quoted on 224).

No, I don't wear a robe and veil! But within our own culture are mores and conventions that apply equally well. Shalit tells about a woman who switched from wearing "spandex, stilettos and skinny cigarette pants" to more modest clothing because she "realized [she] was attracting the wrong kind of man." The "nice" men were apparently too embarrassed by the way she dressed to be seen with her, though they began to notice her and ask her out after she changed her style (224).

I am not going to set up some arbitrary dress code that everyone must follow to be spiritual. The best advice I ever received myself was that a woman's dress should draw attention to her face, where the real person can be seen. Beyond that, perhaps we need to become more attentive to the men around us, finding out what to them seems modest and immodest, respecting their vulnerability. A young married woman once attended a Bible study in our home, and a single man told my husband he would have to stop attending because of the woman's short shorts, which distracted him. I went to talk to her, only to find that she had felt uneasy about her mode of dress, but her husband had approved it and so she suppressed her embarrassment. Yet the most reliable indicator of immodest dress may well be that very sense, if we will listen to it. And the best way to encourage that awareness is to build the "hidden person of the heart" to which Peter refers.

Some women may think these suggestions are old-fashioned and restrictive. "I should be able to wear anything I want; if a man has a problem with it, it's his problem, not mine." But the women I know who dress modestly out of respect for themselves and the men around them find it not constraining but freeing. To honor yourself, to honor your neighbor, to honor God in this way holds its own satisfaction. It also allows us to concentrate on the task at hand, rather than on how men might be responding to our bodies. I am always somewhat amused, as well as saddened, by students who come to class in short skirts and spend the hour tugging at the hems. Why not wear something they can be unself-conscious about in the first place? Fashion should not have such a strong hold over a woman with convictions about the respect she should both give and receive.

Dress, of course, is only one part of modesty. A woman can dress modestly and still be immodest in her speech and behavior, which would surely be the opposite of "a gentle and quiet spirit." This doesn't mean a woman must be a wallflower. Many women are extroverted by nature; they enjoy people and often talk more than less extroverted men (and women), which is not bad in itself. But even an extroverted woman is to avoid the boisterous talk and behavior of the immoral woman (Prov. 7:11), who is a rebel at heart. Boisterousness draws attention to the self, not to the topic of conversation or to others. Sly and flattering speech is also indicted in the immoral woman of Proverbs (5:3; 6:24; 7:21), along with alluring eyes, which might lead some women to reconsider those flirtatious remarks they are in the habit of making. This woman is restless, finding it hard to stay at home and instead "lurking" on street corners looking for action (7:11-12). Although she is married and should be anticipating her husband's return, unmarried women should also consider their motives if they are overly restless themselves, always wanting to go and do in order to be seen—or to avoid quieter occupations (Bible study, volunteer work?) that might lead to spiritual growth.

Immodesty of various sorts seems to be the natural result of feminism, which has created a new sexual double standard. Women like Mary Wollstonecraft and Susan B. Anthony deplored a double standard that allowed men to be promiscuous but condemned women for behavior that might even suggest they were not totally chaste in thought as well as deed. Their solution? Men needed to become chaste. If everyone behaved with modesty, the society would be far better off in every way.

The radical feminists' solution to the problem of the double standard has been a little different: Create a culture in which women are just as free as men to be promiscuous. Absurd perhaps, but, as Shalit documents, successful. It is most difficult for a student living in a public university dorm, for example, to practice chastity. Even if he escapes immoral behavior, it surrounds him, and he cannot escape its assault on his mind and eyes. And now the pendulum has continued its swing. Today women are supposed to be able to do anything they please, go anywhere they please at any time they please, dress however they please; and if a man stares or whistles or touches, he is a boorish jerk. The woman, no matter what, is perfectly innocent and bears no responsibility, they claim.

Of course, a double standard is a double standard whichever party it seems to favor. But even some of our most respected Christian leaders have been sufficiently influenced by the feminism in our culture to preach this double standard at the expense of vilifying men and leaving women ensnared in their sin. We saw how the double standard works in the feminists' wrongheaded insistence that men abuse women, and never the other way around. Let's look at some of the advice given by evangelist Luis Palau concerning sexual sin in his book *Where Is God When Bad Things Happen?*

Palau, who has won many to Christ and usually gives effective scriptural counsel, nonetheless has bought into the new double standard. To Frank, a man whose wife had abandoned him and their ten-year-old son, Palau rightly says that reconciliation must begin with him. Frank needs to submit to Christ and "give to [Him] your sinfulness, your misbehavior, everything you've done that offends God and has brought you to this situation" (115). In other words, turn to God, let Him change your life; then there is hope for the restoration of your marriage. These are appropriate words, even though the wife has obviously sinned in abandoning him, because the only person Frank can change is himself, and his goal should be to restore the marriage. His humility and willingness to admit his faults must be the first step.

In contrast, here is Palau's advice to women whose husbands have left them. He tells Patricia, "You're a young woman, and you have fifty years ahead of you. You can't go on looking back on a man who isn't worth your memories. . . . You will think about him often, but with the help of the Lord, you'll begin to think of him less and less" (113). He then refers to her husband as "some crooked guy who did you in." To Laurie, he says, "You're not perfect, but that's no excuse for your husband to walk out with an old girlfriend" (107).

Of course it's true that the one who leaves is at fault for that sinful choice and shouldn't blame his or her partner for it. But Palau has set up a harmful double standard. A man whose wife leaves him should use it as an opportunity to look at his own sinfulness that might have contributed to the troubled marriage, change with God's help, and seek reconciliation. But a woman whose husband leaves her should take *no* blame on herself, should not look at her own sinfulness, but should forget the "crooked guy" and go on with her life (including possible remarriage, he advises another woman). He tells the women he counsels to forgive their ex-husbands and rid themselves of bitterness; yet his own counsel, it would seem, would at the same time encourage bitterness. He never tells Frank to forgive his wife either or notes her sinfulness in leaving him.

This is hopeless advice for women. If a man should look to himself to see how he contributed to a failing marriage, shouldn't a woman? I've known few instances where a marriage died because of the sin of one partner only. Women aren't perfect. Why should they not be counseled to take stock of themselves and seek reconciliation? I know a woman whose husband left her and their daughter, and that event caused her to humble herself before the Lord, confess her rebellious and independent nature, and then live with hope that he would return. She taught her daughter not to think ill of him, and they prayed together for him for years. When he at last met a Christian man who confronted him with his own sinfulness, the family was reunited and now, many years later, remains a strong witness to the healing power of Jesus Christ. Thank God no one counseled her to "move on" and "forget the crooked guy who did [her] in."

Palau makes the same mistake when he discusses the sin of rape. First let me make clear that there is never an excuse for rape, any more than there is for abandonment or adultery. I'm also aware that rapes occur that could not have been prevented; no woman should feel guilt if that is the case. However, there are rapes that were preventable by the woman, and yet women are being told that they should never feel any guilt whatsoever, no matter what, and are thus being robbed of the chance to evaluate their behavior and attitudes to avoid a reoccurrence.

Let me explain. Date rape, by definition, tells us that a woman has allowed herself to get into a situation where she is vulnerable and many times (though not always) that she has dressed and/or acted in a way that invited sexual attention. I have to admit that I'm amazed at women who dress provocatively, go to a man's apartment alone with him, allow him certain physical liberties, and then complain that he was too aggressive. What did they expect? That a man will be a gentleman when a woman acts like she is sexually available? Of course no woman should be raped, but women must take responsibility for their own actions.

A young woman I know was raped by a former boyfriend. It was a horrible thing, and I wouldn't mind dealing justice to the young man myself. Yet consider the circumstances: She was home by herself after school, neither parent coming home for at least a couple of hours; when he came to the house, she invited him in, not just to the house but into her bedroom. May I be so old-fashioned as to suggest that if she had refused him entrance to the house because she was alone, she would not have been raped?

When we say that a woman bears absolutely no responsibility in such a situation, we are wrong. She had choices, and she made the wrong ones. No, that doesn't excuse the crime or lessen its horror. Yet is it helpful to women to tell them, "You aren't the least responsible, you bear no blame whatsoever" and leave them vulnerable to the same occurrence? It seems to me far more compassionate, while helping the woman to deal with the sin of the man against her, to also lovingly confront her own wrong choices and offer her the possibility of freedom from the same risk at another time.

This is not to say that every time a rape occurs, the woman has contributed to its occurrence. But when she has, she should be held accountable. What, for example, do you say to a young woman who has been repeatedly warned not to run alone in a particular neighborhood and one morning—running alone in that neighborhood—finds herself thrown into the trunk of a maniac's car? Thankfully, this young woman had the presence of mind and courage to open the trunk from the inside and jump from the car, but a loving friend would surely remind her that she had ignored potentially lifesaving advice.

Neither is it helpful to anyone to say that women *ought* to be able to do certain things or go certain places when we know that the reality is that we can't. If I go walk in the park alone at midnight, it doesn't excuse a man for raping me, but it does say something about my foolishness, perhaps even arrogance. And to tell me that I *ought* to be able to walk in the park and I'm not responsible for what happened is robbing me of my dignity and my ability to safeguard myself. We need to realize as well that many of these incidents—date rape, a man abandoning his wife—don't happen in a vacuum. Women in these situations may also be sinful, contributing to the man's selfish desire to sin. *We do not do women a favor by pretending that they are not sinners.*

I am not putting all responsibility for relationships on women. Men have responsibilities too. Yet the reality is that not all men will do what is right; and women should not feel they are always victims, without any power to resist sinful men. Often if we women will do what *we* know is right, men will be constrained to follow our lead. At the least, perhaps we will be able to avoid some of the more uncomfortable or even sinful circumstances that might otherwise occur.

So, women, let's take responsibility for our lives. If we desire a sexual relationship with only one man, we can give ourselves the freedom of acting modestly with all men. We can honor the men around us by not provoking wrong thoughts with our dress, our speech, or our behavior. Then if we encounter harassment of any sort, we can confidently say, "You are wrong; don't treat me that way," and our word will be credible. And if the worst happens, we will be able to avoid the added burden of guilt because of our own sinful behavior and will be better able to understand and accept it as allowed by God, who will bring some good from it if we let Him. Palau tells the story of a missionary woman who was attacked and gang-raped, but who returned to the same place without hostility and won for the Lord the men who had harmed her. He can use all circumstances to help us grow and reach others.

Men and women are all sinners; we solve more problems between us when both sexes are held responsible for their own sins instead of casting blame on each other. Men and women can and should all act modestly toward each other to avoid misunderstandings and worse.

But it is largely the influence of radical secular feminism in our culture that has led to today's permissive and harmful sexual environment. And since this book is directed to women, I want to urge us all to refuse to buy into the lies that tell us we are always victims. If we begin to show respect for both ourselves and the men in our lives, if we honor both God and men in our choices, we can perhaps stem the tide of immorality that is engulfing our society. At the very least, we can stand witness to what *can* be if women care about responsibility, honor, chastity.

The battle of the sexes will be with us until we escape entirely the power of sin when we arrive in heaven. But it needn't be all-consuming nor a continuous, bitter war. Understanding the way God made each of us, respecting and celebrating the differences, honoring the men in our lives, can make the clashes less frequent and more easily resolved in genuine peace instead of a mere uneasy truce.

CHAPTER SEVEN

Motherhood: Still a Sacred Call

Ŝ

When I taught at Southwest Missouri State University, my oldest son, in his early teens then, took some SMSU classes. Every day he'd drop by the Writing Center and give me a big hug. At an age when other boys could hardly bear to admit they had mothers, he gave me public and unself-conscious affection that thrilled my mother's heart. My second son, while in the Army, sent me a necklace laden with symbolism for the love between a mother and son. My daughters faithfully keep in touch with phone calls and cards and gifts of lotions and soaps in pretty bags, something they know I love but won't buy for myself. My youngest son is currently in the "you're the best person in the whole world" phase, and I'm trying not to disillusion him too quickly. At nine he still hugs me often and shows signs that he will remain as affectionate as his older brothers.

These are some of the tangible pluses of motherhood, even for someone who is decidedly *not* "the best person in the whole world," who fails far more than succeeds in mothering, who despairs sometimes over her children's choices, sometimes over her own. But I wouldn't trade any of my children for more peaceful nights and less anxious days. They are all precious gifts from the Lord, of more value than any other earthly gift except their father. They have brought me more joy, more laughter, more love than I could ever have found elsewhere. And the sorrows and the trials and the tears have only made the good that much sweeter.

It doesn't take being a mother to be fully a woman, of course. Many women do not marry, and many married women do not have children; they are just as fully women as any mother. Yet, for many married women who cannot have children, barrenness feels as agonizing as it must have for women like Hannah and Elizabeth, who were even mocked by their contemporaries for their childless state. Today we may not be actually derisive toward the barren woman, but we are often hurtfully insensitive. We ask childless couples when they plan to have children or how long they've been "trying" or if they've considered adoption; we ask them to help with Sunday school and the children's choir without considering how painful such ministries might be for them.

The deep desire for children that most of us have can lead the childless couple to take desperate measures, some of which may be at least questionable ethically. Medical science offers more and more options to "fix" barrenness; but some of these options must be rejected by the Christian couple, such as those that create babies (conveniently called "embryos" or "fertilized eggs") who are later discarded. Other options such as surrogate motherhood and fertilization by the sperm of a man other than the husband should at least give us pause. The mechanisms may be different, but are we not merely practicing the same option as Abraham and Sarah did when they stopped trusting God and used Hagar to conceive a child? Less radical options should be carefully weighed as well, of course.

Where is the line between legitimate medical aid (surgery to correct endometriosis perhaps) and trying to circumvent God's will (some fertility drugs perhaps)?

Primary in these choices must be the couple's submission to God's sovereignty. Is having children the most important aim of marriage, or is it glorifying God? Couples without children may be richly used of Him to minister in ways that neither single people nor people with children can. Perhaps God desires to use their pain to help them reach out to others and comfort them ("with the comfort with which we ourselves are comforted by God," 2 Cor. 1:4); perhaps He will fill their lives with children not biologically their own, either through adoption or ministry. Perhaps a late-in-life baby will provide special joy, comfort, and blessing to them and others.

We do not know the will of God in barrenness, but we know His deep love for each of us. He promises that when we place Him first, we will need to enlarge our tents (see Isa. 54:2) to contain the children He will give us. "The desolate has many more children than she who has a husband," He says (Gal. 4:27); when we acknowledge Him as Lord, He will not let us be ashamed.

May those of us blessed with biological children not forget that our barren sisters may struggle desperately with their desire to be like us. May we remember to show them how much we value their contributions to church and community, the influence of their patience in our lives (what do we wait and yearn for that they remind us to be patient about?). May we uphold them in prayer and learn to know how we can serve and love them.

Of course, many childless women, single and married, serve those of us who are mothers in significant and honoring ways—by baby-sitting, teaching, working in the nursery, and just helping to love those little ones who drain our energy. However, not all women—even those of us with our own children—have the gift of loving and nurturing any number of children anywhere for any reason.

I have always been bemused by the assumption that because I had young children, I must be dying to take care of the nursery during church services or Sunday School, or that I must be eager to help at AWANA—the Scripture memory program many churches run for children—by taking care of the preschool children of the workers. When I was a full-time mom, I certainly didn't have the energy or patience to deal with a large number of other people's children. For a time, when my children were older, I did work in a church nursery because I wished to offer some help to other young mothers, along with giving my daughters an opportunity to "help with the babies," as they kept asking to do.

The experience was good, but not one I am inclined to repeat. In fact, as soon as I discovered I was pregnant with my fifth child, I made my permanent escape from nursery duty. I think young children are adorable, but I am not fitted by nature with the patience to consistently care for several of them at once. This is true of many women I've spoken with, women who, like me, are bemused at the assumption that because they are women they must want to care for large groups of children.

But women, like men, are gifted differently and have different personalities. Some have the gift of singleness and may be called to vocations that have little or nothing to do with children. Some who are married are not given the gift of their own children and may find that circumstance an opportunity to pursue a vocation that could not be pursued if they had children. Some women don't even like young children all that much! One single woman remarked to me after ovarian surgery, "It's just as well it happened to me and not someone else because I have never felt that I wanted children anyway. I'm not comfortable around them."

However, the fact remains that most women wish to and will marry and have children, and mothering will be one of the richest, most fulfilling experiences of their lives. What does the vocation of motherhood entail, and how do we fulfill it in a way that helps our children grow into the kind of adults we hope they will be?

Sadly, today's view of committed motherhood may put off more women than it attracts. Home products are now advertised through commercials that portray women in business suits (instead of the housedresses of the fifties and sixties) going ga-ga over the toilet cleaner that will allow them to spend more time achieving their career goals instead of more time with their families. Movies almost universally portray women in demanding careers whose children are either grown or managing beautifully with a few sentences of parental interaction a day. If the theme is centered on a parent-child conflict, it's usually Dad who's at fault, and Mom's absence from the family has nothing to do with it. Single working moms also abound, but seldom do we see the stay-at-home mom. Thanks to Betty Friedan and the radical feminists, the general cultural consensus—almost as much within the church as without—is that motherhood is something to be either avoided or, if she "wants it all," fitted in around a woman's all-important career.

Indeed, the need for a career for personal fulfillment has been so elevated that many women return to work within a week or two of giving birth, leaving their infants to be raised by caretakers they hardly even know. Many women whose families don't need a second income apparently believe that a low-paid, boring job is better than being "just a housewife," even when their children are young. Certainly I've met a fair number of

women, many in the church, who seem baffled by my desire to
stay at home rather than hold a job, especially when they realize that I genuinely love teaching.

Don't misunderstand me. I am not going to say that no
mother should ever, under any circumstances, hold a paying
job outside the home while her children are young.
Circumstances vary. I have worked full-time in a demanding
profession all of my youngest child's life and most of my older
children's as well, not by choice but by necessity. I know a man
who is a professional writer, and his wife is a physician; her job
allows him to pursue his with financial security for the family,
and his allows a parent to be home with their young child, a
far better option than child care. However, more and more
women are returning home to be committed mothers, the primary influence in their children's lives as they grow up. And
Scripture shows us the influence of mothers, negative as well
as positive, along with the honor in which God holds mothers—a good antidote to the modern cultural view that motherhood isn't really very important.

If we are inclined to believe that mothers are not especially
significant in their children's lives, perhaps we should remember
the favoritism of Rebekah, which led her to aid Jacob in deceiv-
ing his father, tearing apart family ties and surely contributing
to Jacob's own favoritism that sowed discontent among his sons.
Righteous Asa apparently overcame the idolatrous influence of
his mother, but he removed her from her position as queen to
limit her wide national influence (2 Chron. 15). Athaliah,
mother of Azariah, counseled her son to do evil, and in the one
year of his reign he ruled in the manner of Ahab, the most
wicked of all the kings of Israel (2 Chron. 22). And Herodias
used her daughter to orchestrate the death of John the Baptist.

But if mothers have influence for evil, of course they have

influence for good as well. There is Mary, who listened for God's voice, sacrificed her reputation for the sake of her Child, treasured and pondered the prophecies concerning her Son, exercised authority over Him and taught Him while He was young, ministered to Him when He was an adult, and wept for Him at the foot of the cross. I think of Naomi and how she loved a daughter-in-law to salvation, helped her secure her future, and was rewarded with grandchildren as dear to her as if they had been her son's children. Remember Hannah, too, so desperate for a son that she was willing to part with him at a very young age so he could serve God fully. How well she must have trained him the first few years of his life in light of God using him so mightily, even when he was afterwards raised by a man who had failed to give proper direction and discipline to his own sons. And of course there are Timothy's mother and grandmother, who faithfully taught him the Word and the love of God, fitting him for his ministry as an elder in the church.

God certainly holds mothers in high esteem. One of the ten commandments, of course, demands that children honor mothers along with fathers. The law repeatedly reminded the Israelites that to dishonor one's parents in any way is a capital crime, i.e., punishable by death: "he who strikes his father or his mother" (Exod. 21:15); he who curses either father or mother (Lev. 20:9); he who won't listen to either father or mother—both of whom have "chastened" him (Deut. 21:18-21). The child who "setteth light" (disgraces, shames, despises, or lightly esteems) either father or mother (Deut. 27:16, KJV) will be cursed by God. Jesus honored His mother by remaining in obedience to her (Luke 2:51) and also by making provision for her future even as He hung dying on the cross (John 19:26-27). He did not raise many people from death, but one was the only son of a widow, on whom He took compassion surely not merely because of the emotional tragedy but also because without her son's support she might well have been cast into poverty.

Furthermore, God does not hesitate to use the imagery of motherhood to describe Himself to us. He is like a hen wishing to bring Israel under the safety of His wings; He will nurture and comfort His children as a mother (Isa. 66:9-11). When David says he is calm as "a weaned child," the image is that of a child resting quietly in his mother's arms (Ps. 131:2). Wisdom—personified as a woman in Proverbs and equated by some commentators with Jesus Christ—cries out to her children to listen to her (Prov. 8:32).

Mothers have always been important, and they are no less so now than in Bible times. Committed mothers make a difference in their children's lives; and so, sadly, do mothers who choose not to find the time to be committed to their children. To be mothers means to give our lives to our children, the same as every vocation requires—the sacrifice of self. Of course, this is not entirely possible on our own. Remember that Luther says vocation does two things: It keeps the world functioning in some kind of order even among unbelievers, and it shows us that we do not have the ability to meet all the requirements of our various callings in our own strength. As we turn to God, first for salvation and then for power in our daily living, we understand that He accomplishes His will through even our imperfect exercise of vocation.

Consider both parenthood and childhood as vocations, marked by particular behaviors expected of each. The child's vocation is marked by obedience to and respect of authority: "Obey your parents in all things, for this is well pleasing to the Lord"; "'Honor your father and mother . . . that . . . you may live long on the earth'" (Col. 3:20; Eph. 6:2-3). The parents' vocation is marked by the command to train up our children "in

the training and admonition of the Lord" (Eph. 6:4)—to teach
them a proper regard for both earthly authority and the authority of God. As we do these things, not out of duty but out of love
for God and each other, as we do them in the power of the Holy
Spirit instead of in our own inadequate fleshly power, we begin
to understand and see the results of God's work. It is now God
Himself, living in us, who teaches and trains our children; we see
that our human failures can be forgiven and mitigated by His
love and work in their lives. This is a point well worth keeping
in mind as we explore some of the practical ways we train our
children by modeling proper submission to our various authorities and by directly teaching and training our children.

If neither father nor mother is with the children most of the
time throughout at least their early years, who is shaping their
values? All too often it is other children in a busy day-care situation, or a caretaker who may not share the same values as the
parents. If a father is home through necessity or choice, the situation is far better. However, a mother's care and attention differs from a father's, and when she is not at home, for whatever
reason, there is a price to pay. Understanding what motherhood
entails may be the first step toward making that price as low as
possible when it must be incurred.

Where better to start looking for a picture of motherhood
than Proverbs 31, whose ideal woman has a husband who trusts
her and children who "rise up and call her blessed." I admit that
I was startled when I first discovered that there is no explicit reference to this woman's mothering. And yet for her children to
honor her so completely, she must have been most involved in
their lives. Consider her many activities, in all of which, by the
way, she pleases her husband: feeding and clothing her household, including the servants (no small thing in the days before
frozen dinners and Wal-Mart); making cloth and garments to

sell; assessing and buying property, then supervising its productive use; visiting and aiding the poor. No wonder she "does not
eat the bread of idleness"!

So when in all this busyness did she mother? How did she
raise children who would bless her in their adulthood?

Not by putting them into day care and public school or handing them over full-time to the servants while she went out and
"fulfilled herself." Rather, she "watches over the ways of her
household," and that includes the children. And while the
extended household no doubt helped in her labors, I believe we
can safely assume that her children were with her much of the
time, learning from toddlerhood to help, observing her kind and
patient spirit, imbibing her wisdom. Clearly she did not center
her life around her children, but they must have been an integral
part of all she did.

Here is an important lesson for today's culture. One thing
that we don't want to do is be *solely* mothers, living for and
through our children. This seems to be at least one root of the
cultural problems that began after World War II and perhaps a
source of the demeaning image we so frequently see of the
housewife. Until that time, children were children—helping the
family in a variety of ways, sometimes including a job meant to
help the family as a whole—until they became young adults,
generally marked by sexual maturity and marriage.
"Adolescence," with its unhealthy focus on the child's self-centered comfort, was not an official stage of the growth process as
it is now. In a *World Magazine* article, "Warning: The 50s Led
to the 60s," Frederica Mathewes-Green discusses the desire to
re-create a fantasized "golden age" after the horrors of war,
which seems to have sent many women home with the notion
that it was their responsibility to create perfect havens for their
families by living at the beck and call of spouse and especially

children. "We don't want them to have to work the way we did," the parents of this newly materialistic and wealthy society said; "we want them to enjoy their youth."

Now, I hardly advocate taking five-year-olds and putting them in the coal mines. However, we have gone so far the other direction that it seems to some people cruel to ask a perfectly capable five-year-old to pick up the toys he has strewn about the house, or a teenager to wash the dishes before taking off for the mall. Women were never meant to be slaves to their children; we are meant to be adults who teach our children how to become adults—thinking of others instead of only themselves, learning to serve instead of demanding to be served, and beginning to understand their place in God's scheme of things.

This, in fact, is one point Betty Friedan got right. She discusses at some length research that showed that many young men, children of the fifties, my generation, did not seem to understand how to be men. They fell apart under military discipline; they related to their wives more as surrogate mothers than as wives; they suffered from various psychological disorders. Many psychologists traced these problems directly to the coddling of mothers who "lived for" their children (especially their sons) and didn't help them grow up to take their places as individuals able to function within society (190-192).

Of course, we cannot solve the problem of too much attention of the wrong kind by chasing the opposite extreme and claiming that a few hurried minutes of contact in a day is sufficient, as happens in far too many of our modern families. Proverbs 31 seems to suggest a balance: training children to become adults by involving them intimately in the daily routine of the family, meeting the family's needs and goals instead of catering to any individual(s) within it. Whatever the particular circumstances of each family, we must remember that it takes time and effort to "bring [children] up in the training and admonition of the Lord" (Eph. 6:4).

And this training of children is not an easy task. Often it seems that no matter how badly some people do it, their children turn out well, and no matter how well others do it, their children turn out badly. Yet we must do our best before the Lord and understand that the ultimate decisions about their lives are up to our children themselves; we can only provide the best foundation for their choices that we can and pray that they will choose to build upon that foundation.

The story of Eli offers what seems to me a basic principle in raising children: More than just teaching is vital if we want children to follow the path of righteousness; we must also model righteousness ourselves and train our children to obey our word so they will obey God's. As a priest who was raising his sons for the priesthood, Eli obviously taught his sons the law of God. However, they used their office as a means to self-gratification, taking the fat of the sacrifices that was supposed to be burnt before the Lord, fornicating with the women who gathered at the temple, and leading the people astray (1 Sam. 2:16, 22, 24). When Eli heard of this, he rebuked them but did not put a stop to their immoralities. God sent a prophet to tell Eli that his family would be cut off from Israel because of the sins of his sons— and his own sin in honoring them above God, a sin that modeled for his sons the unrighteous pursuit of self (1 Sam. 2:29). Later, through Samuel, the prophecy was confirmed, with the added rebuke that Eli's sin lay in not "restrain[ing]" his sons (1 Sam. 3:13). He did not insist on their *doing* what was right and *avoiding* what was evil; he did not, in other words, *train* them in the path but only *told* them of it.

Fathers and mothers share the responsibilities and results of teaching and training. The instruction of each is to be equally heeded and respected, as several verses in Proverbs attest. "My son," the writer admonishes, "hear the instruction of your father, and do not forsake the law of your mother" (1:8). "Listen to your father who begot you, and do not despise your mother when she is old" (23:22). Mothers and fathers share equally in the joy of godly children: "The father of the righteous will greatly rejoice, and he who begets a wise child will delight in him. Let your father and mother be glad, and let her who bore you rejoice" (23:24-25). They also share equally in the shame of rebellious children: "A foolish son is a grief to his father, and bitterness to her who bore him" (17:25). Proverbs 6:20, 23, tell the son to "keep" his "father's command" and to "not forsake" his mother's "law," because "the commandment is a lamp, and the law a light" and by their means he can avoid the snare of the immoral woman.

These verses are actually directed to children; we understand the parents' responsibility from them through implication. Clearly, parents are to teach; but children are to obey, to give their parents reason to rejoice in them through the obedience and wisdom they display as they mature. In like manner, God expects us to mature into wisdom as His children, causing Him to rejoice over us when we do, or to grieve when we rebel. A friend recently e-mailed me a desperate plea for prayer. Her oldest son, she had been told, had slipped further into ungodly patterns that now threatened his schooling and career goals. The grief in her words made my own heart ache. But what rejoicing a day later to find that the information given was incorrect, and the young man had in fact just made choices to live his life fully for his Lord. So closely juxtaposed, those emotions brought home to me the importance of my vocation as mother—and gratefulness that all doesn't depend on my halting, human attempts, for God is the One who brings the fruit.

Yet we must of course be faithful to our trust. As we are reminded in Deuteronomy 6:7, we are to teach continually: "You shall teach [My words] diligently to your children, and shall talk of them when you sit in your house, when you walk by the way, when you lie down, and when you rise up." The command is given to all Israel—and therefore to both fathers and mothers. But how can it be obeyed if interaction between parents and children is limited to a few minutes per day?

The Israelites did, after all, live in a very different culture from ours. Mothers primarily taught both boys and girls until the sons were old enough to begin learning their father's trade and attending school to learn the Torah. The entire family often spent many more hours daily in each other's presence than many modern families in our industrialized culture do in a week or a month. It was much easier, then, in that culture to work together as parents to teach and train the children, to instill in them obedience to God's commands in daily practice, for mother and father both to "teach [the Word] diligently," day in and day out.

Today we must make a special effort to find ways to obey this command. Many parents place their children in Christian schools where their beliefs and values are not only respected but actively taught. (A caution, however: Research the local Christian school carefully, as not all teach what you might expect.) Families who place their children into the public school system are the hardest pressed as they seek consistent time to impress the Word on their children, to talk with them about the happenings of their day and help them understand the practical application of the Word to those happenings, to offset the constant bombardment of a secular worldview in their children's lives. If both parents are working full-time outside the home, finding consistent time to do this is an even greater challenge than if the mother is available—emotionally as well as physically—when school is out.

I recall a friend a number of years ago describing a typical day to me: get her two young boys (preschool and early elementary) up early, nag them to eat quickly and get dressed so she could get them to the sitter and be on time to work; work long hours in an exhausting job, often taking on overtime; hurry to the baby-sitter's after work to collect the boys, who had returned there after school was out; run any necessary errands, such as grocery shopping, while trying to listen to the chatter of her children—difficult enough at any time but especially so when she was tired from dealing with people all day and trying to make decisions about her errands; try to get dinner on the table before her husband arrived home, not letting the boys help because there wasn't time, but instead sending them off to their room to play; throw a load of laundry in; hurry the boys into pajamas and into bed, often without a story or other ritual because of the need to rise early the next morning and start over again; the sharp rebukes and angry discipline she would fall into from sheer frustration. "There's no such thing as quality time," she told me, "without quantity." More and more families are beginning to understand this.

More and more women, and not just Christian women, are coming home to care for their children and are learning to manage a family on a single income. The strongest incentive, of course, is the simple realization that no one can take care of their children as well as they themselves can. For Christian families, the desire to take seriously God's command to teach their children diligently and continually is often at the heart of this decision, especially as the surrounding culture becomes more secularized daily. Many of these families are further choosing to educate their children at home for the same reason: Why spend so much time debriefing when you can teach the truth in the first place? And a growing number of these families are also creating home businesses so both parents can be involved in daily teaching and training the children, and so the children can learn from an early age the various responsibilities inherent in supporting a family—much as was common for families prior to the Industrial Revolution, which, as we saw earlier, took much meaningful work out of the home.

There are, of course, families who can't choose these options—single parents, for example, and those who honestly can't live on a single income (though some who claim this should perhaps reassess their priorities to determine the difference between needs and desires). For these same families, private Christian schools may not be an option because of the expense. I can only say to them that God knows their circumstances, and He offers sufficient grace to cope with them.

I know single mothers who diligently involve extended and/or church family in their lives so their children will have the influence of godly men and can see how intact families function. When child care is necessary, parents who are concerned about their children's moral and spiritual growth seek out the best available—extended family, church care, or day care with a very small adult-child ratio where their values will be upheld. Making time to truly listen and be available, as my friend discovered, is extremely difficult, yet vital to a child's security. Some families insist on at least one meal a day together. Parents can sacrifice overtime or some of their own leisure to attend games, concerts, recitals, science fairs—whatever their children are involved in. When adults do this graciously, it makes it much easier for children to be willing to make some sacrifices as well. (Often children are too involved outside the home and family themselves; our example can help them find balance.)

Whatever the circumstances, the command applies: We are to diligently teach our children the Word of God. We must make time to do this; we can't count solely on church attendance and a daily devotion—important though these are—to be sufficient. But the command also implies that teaching alone is not enough; if we are doing this at all times—when we sit and walk and lie down and rise up—then we are to be training our children to obey the Word we are teaching by our own obedience and by our insistence on theirs.

Parents who live by the philosophy "do as I say, not as I do" are bound to lose both the respect and the obedience of their children. Modeling righteous behavior is vitally important in the raising of our children. Mothers must demonstrate a godly submission to our husbands (see Chapters 4 and 6 for discussion of this issue) if we desire the obedience of our children. Also, we must demonstrate in our daily lives submission to Scripture, church authority, and an employer if we work outside the home. Of course, none of us will be perfect, but when we fall short we have the opportunity to model confession and repentance to our sons and daughters.

The choices we make day by day offer excellent opportunities to model and teach at the same time. In making decisions about large purchases, for example, we can discuss the principles involved in the presence of our children: Is the item an actual need? Do we have enough money to buy it without jeopardizing more important needs or going into debt? Are there alternatives to purchasing, such as renting or borrowing, that would serve our need? We invite the children to pray with us for wisdom and involve them in research to determine the best buy. No need to preach sermons—we simply go about the process, perhaps pausing to explain the scriptural basis for a particular principle we are applying.

It doesn't always "take," of course. I recently heard a young adult remark about a sibling, "I can't understand why he doesn't have any money sense! It's not like our parents didn't show us how important it is all our lives!" Personality traits differ among children, making each more prone to apply some instruction and ignore some other, and rebellion shows up in different areas too. And as Eli's example shows us, teaching isn't enough, even when combined with modeling (he did give his sons a righteous example in some areas). Training is necessary as well.

It is important to remember that even when the teaching and modeling are combined with insistence on appropriate behavior, some children will decline to live righteously when allowed to make their own choices. However, without all three, the chances of raising righteous children plummet. Training makes the Word and our example begin to take root in their lives, giving them the experience of righteous action.

Proverbs 29:15 warns us that "a child left to himself brings shame to his mother," the only verse that refers solely to the effect of the mother neglecting to discipline her children. (Other verses talk about how the foolish child breaks the hearts of mother and father.) Perhaps this is because while both parents must be involved in training their child, the mother is usually the one responsible for the greater amount, as she is with the child more hours of the day. Or perhaps it simply means that her more emotional nature causes her to feel the shame more deeply. But why this particular warning to mothers about leaving a child "to himself"?

While it is not a universal characteristic, mothers do tend to have a more sympathetic view of their children; it is often harder for a tenderhearted mother to discipline a child than for her husband to do so. And it is always more difficult to be consistent in discipline when we are with a child for hours on end. When I had four children under the age of six, such discipline seemed at times impossible from sheer weariness. I had to repent of not disciplining at all at least as often as of disciplining in anger. But I found that when I disciplined consistently—and made as few rules as possible—the children were more consistently obedient, and I was not as tempted to make angry responses. The diligence that God commands, which I had understood to be for my children's benefit, also made my job easier in the long run.

Mothers also have many distractions as they go about their daily work, another temptation to overlook the need for discipline. When right in the middle of stirring the gravy or sewing a seam or writing an article, it is all too easy to say something to a disobedient child but do nothing, thus losing credibility and causing the child to keep seeking the limits. Elisabeth Elliot shares in *Let Me Be a Woman* (letters she wrote to her engaged daughter) about the need for attention in training a child. "I had many things on my mind in the running of a jungle mission station," she writes to Valerie. "I was sometimes tempted to pay little attention to your small needs. You knew it at once. You knew whether it was an opportune time to get away with something. You would try it, and my preoccupied, 'Val, leave that alone,' you would ignore. You knew you could safely ignore it because my attention had already turned back to the thing at hand." But as she learned to give Valerie her full attention when speaking to her, the child's attitude would change. "Your eyes would open wide when I stopped what I was doing and looked at you. Slowly, slowly, your hand would drop when I said your name. . . . Either I meant it or I did not, and there was no dissimulating with you" (44-45). Our children must understand that we will hold them accountable for disobedience if we wish them to obey other authorities in their lives.

Because of our frequent tiredness and distraction, along with a tender nature that desires to maintain harmony, I think we moms tend to learn early on that it's much easier—at least at the moment—to do things ourselves and give in to our children's demands. It is much harder to train a child to do an excellent job of any household chore than to do it ourselves. Once a friend remarked to me after dinner at the home of a church elder, "At first I was put off during dinner because my silver wasn't completely clean. Then when I saw the kids get up and cheerfully clear the table and wash the dishes, I realized it was a small price to pay for the discipline they're learning." And the freedom that their mother gained as they took on some of the household chores allowed her to minister more directly to their guests.

As a mother who works outside the home, I have often felt guilty about not spending more time with my children. It is especially difficult now that all the older children are gone and the nine-year-old, who is extremely extroverted, begs for attention in various ways. Recently he requested that I tell him a story when I put him to bed. Earlier I had read to him, and we had agreed that the reading would take the place of bedtime stories. So I said no, reminding him that I was sick and had a lot of papers to grade before I could go to sleep. As he began to object, I said, "Mommy loves you."

"No, you don't," he answered; "you won't read me a story."

I was sorely tempted at that point to give in. Certainly it would have saved time and emotional energy. However, a much more important issue was at stake than my comfort—his need to respect our agreement and my circumstances. After I reminded him the world did not revolve around him, we talked and prayed that he would repent of his selfish and disrespectful demand. I consider this a particularly important lesson for our sons because it may be partially through our own weakness that we help breed disrespect for women in general. Often I find that my children are willing to whine or argue with me about issues they would never dare to argue about with their dad, and it is only immediate discipline that convinces them I am not to be manipulated and treated disrespectfully. We must learn the fine line between the empathy and tenderness we may naturally have and the desire for peace that causes us to back down from needed discipline.

But a mother's empathy and tenderness also lead her to be more alert to problems that others might miss, and to deal with them in a way that sympathizes with a child's frustration while leading him to a solution for it. I am most blessed to work with some of my child's AWANA leaders, and one day two colleagues, at different times, mentioned to me a display of anger on his part during the game time, which they said he'd gotten over. However, I know his ability to move on without really dealing with an emotion; so I asked him about it when I got home that evening. Sure enough, he still felt angry, because he thought a leader had been unfair. Because I had been aware for some time of his desire for fair play, a perfect opportunity opened to discuss with him the purpose of rules in games, the imperfections of those who judge the games, and his responsibilities to always play by the rules and to accept the judgments gracefully, even when they are imperfect. I hadn't realized that he was ready for these more abstract concepts, but he has seemed to be happier and more content in his play since then.

Mothers have a particular responsibility toward their daughters, to take joy in being women and to show them the path toward developing "a gentle and quiet spirit, which is very precious in the sight of God" (1 Pet. 3:4). As I mentioned earlier, I found myself appalled at the immodest dress of junior high and high school girls in one church we attended—until I saw the dress of their mothers. If we are not modest, we cannot hope for our daughters to be; after all, they may not choose to be even if we are. When mothers chafe at housework and show clear irritation and annoyance at how long it takes their children to do their chores, how can we expect our daughters to be contented to be someone's helpmeet? Perhaps one of the most joyful moments of my life was my older daughter's phone call to tell me she was engaged. "All I've ever wanted is to be a wife and mom," she told me. "I plan to stay home when we have children." As difficult as it's been to be an example to her because of our circumstances, and as often as I have failed in my own walk as a woman, those words thrilled my soul and made me thankful once again for my mother's influence, because she has shown so much of godly womanhood to my children.

Teaching, modeling, training—these are the guidelines to lay a godly foundation in our children's lives, which we then pray they will choose to build upon. The father's commandment and the mother's law, when a child pays heed to them, are like "an ornament of grace . . . and chains about your neck" (Prov. 1:6); we thus fulfill our vocation to our children to make them beautiful in the sight of God and of the world. It is not easy, but He promises that He is the One working through us when we are willing to sacrifice ourselves for the sake of the ones He has entrusted to our care for a little time.

CHAPTER EIGHT

Women and Wages

ᔥ

We have seen how modern feminists insist that women need careers for self-fulfillment, to the extent that they are sometimes even hostile to women who choose to stay at home, considering them leeches and fools. Yet the true source of self-fulfillment is the loss of self in service to Christ and neighbor, not the seeking of the self in jobs or worldly acclaim—or in housewifery, for that matter. Anything can become an idol to us fallen people, and if we feel discontentment making us restless, it is probably time to check our motives before trying to change our circumstances.

It is true that most women work for wages at some point in their lives, though the statistics used by feminists are rather misleading. They would have us believe that most women work in full-time jobs outside the home, whether by choice or necessity. Yet the figures they use include all women who have worked for pay for any length of time at all; thus a woman who helps take the census but does no other paid work during the year is included as a "working woman." So is the woman who takes a part-time job for extra money at Christmas, or the woman who does part-time work from her home. The truth is that the majority of married women with children still spend most of their time as homemakers, and they do so because they want to place their children first (Loveless).

Also, an increasing number of women professionals are choosing to come home to raise their children. Every year I read more stories like that of a woman I know who held a prestigious engineering position and gave it up because she wanted better for her boys than day care and public schooling could give them. Invariably these women say that their children need *them*, not a caregiver who can never love them as a mother does, and that they themselves want to experience real motherhood, which they find more satisfying than all the worldly accolades they might have previously received.

The single woman considering her future would do well to keep these facts in mind. Does she want to enter a career that will demand consistent full-time work in order to advance? Is she reasonably certain she wants to marry and have children at some point? The future, of course, is not entirely in our own hands, and even women who want to marry won't always do so; but if she strongly desires a family, it might be well to plan her career with that in mind.

I recall being most upset with a male colleague some years ago who told me about his annoyance with a particularly bright female student. She had come to college planning to be a doctor and had the ability to do so, but as her graduation drew near she changed her career plans. She would become a physician's assistant instead, she told him, because she wanted a family someday, and a doctor has to spend too much time away from home. My colleague was annoyed because she was "wasting her mind" by not pursuing a medical degree. I was thrilled that she placed family as a higher priority and was upset that Christian professors were demeaning that choice. Not that I think Christian women shouldn't be doctors—I seek out godly women doctors myself. But why should we ever tell a particular woman that her desire to place family above career is a waste of her mind?

My older daughter openly shared her hopes for marriage and family and her intention to stay home with her children someday, only to be looked on as something of a freak by her coworkers. "They're always giving me advice about how I need to keep working and get into a better job," she told me once. "But I just want to be a mom."

I think she's been making wise choices, since that is her heart desire. Before she became engaged, she was saving money for college and taking every opportunity offered her at work to become more knowledgeable and skilled. And now that she's married, she still plans to get a degree in her chosen field—counseling—which she can use full-time or part-time or take a break from indefinitely. If something happens to her husband, she will have skills with which to support a family, but she won't be locked into work that requires continuous employment for success.

It seems to me there are two main mistakes I see single women making. One is to make an idol of a career, assuming it is their means to self-fulfillment; as a result, they pursue career goals so zealously that they end up with an agonizing choice between career and family at some later time (or miss out on the joy of family altogether). The other error is to make an idol of marriage, assuming they must and will marry in order to be fulfilled, thus setting themselves up to be bitter old maids or, perhaps worse, bitter wives when marriage turns out not to be as ideal as they had expected. These women may also avoid developing their gifts and abilities as fully as they could.

So perhaps the best thing I know to say to single women is simply this: Put your trust in your Lord, who knows your needs and desires and already knows what your future holds. Rather than looking to either work or marriage as your means to self-fulfillment, remember that you find yourself only as you lose yourself in service. And here we encounter the doctrine of vocation once again: Vocation is our service to our neighbor, and the vocations we exercise will depend on the circumstances in which we find ourselves, circumstances that tend to change over time and may turn out to be quite different from what we had planned, as mine, for example, have.

James's exhortation may help in this matter of deciding what to do with our lives. He rebukes those who say, "Today or tomorrow we will go to such and such a city, spend a year there, buy and sell, and make a profit" because they are presuming upon the future by assuming they will even be alive tomorrow to accomplish their plans. Yet he doesn't say *not* to make plans because we don't know the future; rather, he says to be humble about them: "Instead you ought to say, 'If the Lord wills, we shall live and do this or that'" (James 4:13-17).

So the single woman should humbly pursue the goals on her heart, yet know that God may change those goals at any time He sees fit and thus be willing to move in a new direction as He leads. If your heart desire is to serve, using your unique gifts in the context of your womanhood, God will lead you to the decisions concerning work that will most benefit you, too, in the long run. Remember, God's desire is "to give you a future and a hope" (Jer. 29:11).

Know, too, that where God leads you may not be where others go—or where others think you should go. "A man's heart plans his way, but the LORD directs his steps" (Prov. 16:9). If the Lord directs you to a full-time intensive career such as medicine, by all means go! If He directs you to be a full-time wife and mother, by all means go! If you find your self-worth in His love for you, you will be content wherever He leads, finding the fullness of life He intends for you, no matter what others' choices are or how they feel about yours. And remember that His direction may change with the various stages of life most women experience—singlehood, marriage, young children, older children, the "empty nest," grandchildren . . . In all of life He is the one constant.

For married women the questions about paid work are somewhat different. Before children come, whatever the husband and wife agree on is obviously fine. Some women may prefer not to work outside the home because they have interests better pursued with a free schedule—volunteer work or a neighborhood ministry, for example. Others may wish to bolster the savings account before children take them out of the workforce. This may be a good time for some to establish a freelance career that can be adjusted to the varying needs of the family over the years.

After children come into the family, the question of a mother's working for pay becomes much more serious, as the welfare of children cannot be assured in just any setting. Of course, for women whose husbands don't make a family wage, working may be the only option. However, couples facing this apparent necessity should take a long hard look at their financial situation and their lifestyle. In my case, we have always lived on one wage, which has been under the official U.S. "poverty" level for most of our marriage; yet we have never lacked for food, clothing, shelter, and a vehicle. Granted, at times the food was monotonous, the clothing mostly came from garage sales or the Salvation Army, the shelter was sometimes not the most spacious or best located, and the vehicles . . . well, let's just say that on the dash of one we taped the verse "In Him all things hold together" and prayed over it every time we needed to go somewhere!

Eventually, it's true, we were given certain loans and gifts by our parents that have helped us establish ourselves in a home debt-free. But during those early years we found we could live well on far less than many couples (and our government, apparently) think is possible, simply because our reasons for doing so—having one parent at home and a commitment to stay out of debt—were compelling enough to sacrifice many amenities others think are necessary.

I could tell story after story of men working more than one job or couples both working, making far more than we do but never seeming to have enough. I know one man with an excellent faculty position at a state university, plus a hefty military reserve wage, who still worked odd jobs and whose wife took on baby-sitting because they "couldn't make ends meet." Yet they bought all new clothing for their children, paying exorbitant prices for clothes that hardly look worn after they're outgrown, insisted on having two cars and a luxurious home, wouldn't hear of buying secondhand appliances, and spent more on groceries for a family of three than we did for a family of six. True, this mother was home with their children, but at what cost to her husband, who hardly had time to see them?

I know there are people with jobs whose wages won't support a family. But there are many families who think this is true when the reality is that their sense of "need" is out of balance. More and more families are finding that raising their own children is worth sacrificing the world's luxuries—the more so when a close look at where the second salary goes often reveals that a large portion of it is merely paying for the expenses incurred solely because of the second job: clothing, car expenses, taxes, meals, day care, etc. The remainder can often be made up for by practicing greater economy and/or lowering our desire for material goods.

My heart goes out to those women who must work so the bills can be paid; they are not usually the ones with the high-paying, prestigious jobs and often would prefer to be home. God understands the needs of every family, however. A study once showed that children of single parents who are widowed suffered fewer ill effects than children of single parents who are divorced. Though the needs remain the same, I believe God pours out more grace to those whose less-than-ideal circumstances have come about by necessity rather than selfish choices. (As James says, quoting from Proverbs, "God resists the proud, but gives grace to the humble" [4:6]). The attitudes of parents will be different too, of course. Children can tell the difference between a mother whose heart is with them no matter how much time she has and a mother who sees them as far down her priority list for selfish reasons.

We do know that it is difficult to find good day care for preschool children. The best care, of course, would be given by extended family such as grandparents, who love the children the same way the parents do, generally hold the same values, and can give them the attention they need. Second best would be placement with someone who baby-sits only a few children in her home—perhaps an older church member or another mom.

If children must be placed in a day-care center, beyond the health and safety concerns that any parent would check out, it's also important to have a very small adult to child ratio in which every child is guaranteed a substantial amount of adult contact each day. This is vitally important for two reasons: language development and social development. Children under five in particular must be extensively exposed to adult language usage if they are to become fluent in their native language. The same applies to social development; adult examples of interaction are vital for maturity. These same issues must be considered by mothers who don't *have* to work outside the home but may wish to do so.

If a woman's desire to work outside the home is based on the false idea disseminated by the feminists that she needs to make money in order to have self-esteem, she particularly needs to reconsider, first, where self-esteem really comes from, which has already been discussed; and second, whether the so-called advantages of work really are advantages when compared to homemaking and child-rearing.

One issue that we looked at earlier is the effect of the Industrial Revolution on women's work in the home. When virtually all of a family's needs were met within the home, women had plenty of varied and creative tasks to fill their time. However, much of this work was lost to the factories of the Industrial Revolution. According to Mary Stewart Van Leeuwen, this turned the home into "merely a unit for consuming things produced elsewhere," making women "unwaged consumers and caretakers" who no longer shared "economic productivity" with their husbands (200). This is the reason Betty Friedan was so adamant that a woman must have a career: "She can find identity only in work that is of real value to society—work for which, usually, our society pays" (346). Even when their wages were not needed, she says, women who worked for pay "earned tangible proof of their ability to contribute" (376). Thus the loss of economic production is equated with the loss of a sense of fulfillment, of self-esteem, for women at home.

Let's look a little more closely at the situation.

The greatest economic and family effects of the Industrial Revolution first influenced rural families. As many of the products they had traditionally made for themselves and sold in cottage industries became factory-made and cheaper, the large and wealthy landowners began buying up more land, and freeholders became employees of the wealthy or moved to the cities. In either situation, they could no longer fully support themselves with the produce of their own land but had to have ready cash to buy what they formerly made. But the husband could rarely make enough to support the family's new needs; so women and children were forced into factories and sweatshops and their appalling conditions to supplement the husband's wage. These women were not the feminists of the day—they didn't have time to be.

Rather, middle-class women were the feminists. Feminism has always been a luxury only the middle and upper class could afford. The Industrial Revolution had rather less effect on middle-class women; the shopowner or tradesman could generally make a family wage (with his family usually helping him, just as the farmer's family had always helped on the farm). The effects were slower and not nearly as horrific as for the poor. In fact, one of the causes the early feminists took on was labor reform to protect poor women and children from the exploitation of the factory owners, as well as reform of other laws to benefit poor women abused by husbands and employers, to reduce the incidence of prostitution, etc. This concern for the poor and the displaced was a hallmark of early feminism—as contrasted to modern feminism, in which middle- and upper-class women pay poorer women low wages to do the "demeaning" care of their children and homes while they "fulfill themselves" in prestigious and high-paying careers.

Once the goals of the early feminists had been met—the vote, entrance to colleges and professions, legal reforms of the sort mentioned above—the women's movement really died out for some time. Women could pretty much do what they wanted, but many still stayed home with their children. It was, as we have seen, Friedan's *The Feminine Mystique* that started the modern feminist movement. Obviously she hit a nerve with many discontented housewives who wanted more out of life than they had.

But was the problem that they had become "passive consumers" and were not contributing to the economic needs of the family? If so, how do we account for the many, many women like my mother, who never worked for a wage but has been busy and content for some fifty-seven years of marriage? The problem for the women Friedan described, as discussed in Chapter 3 of this book, has much more to do with not having a purpose beyond selfish satisfaction. Careers ultimately don't solve that problem any more than housewifery does.

I am disturbed by the refrain that women who don't work for a wage are merely "passive consumers" and therefore lack self-esteem. My mother and the mothers of my friends were not "passive consumers" sitting around watching soap operas all day. Laborsaving devices and the purchasing of many of the things previously made in the home did not make their lives empty and worthless. They contributed actively to the total welfare of the home by their physical care of it, by their wise use of the wages earned by their husbands (which was always "our" money, not "his"), by their baking and sewing, gardening and canning. They were left with more time, yes, and used that time for church work and charities, for helping in their children's schools and attending their children's activities, for developing friendships with other women and supporting each other in times of need. These women had self-esteem because they did not live for themselves. And their husbands did not look on them as leeches!

Yes, the Industrial Revolution contributed to a very different culture—and one that is not necessarily better in every way. But it was only one influence among many, including a materialist and relativist philosophy that—more than the lack of "meaningful work"—caused the discontentment of women in the sixties.

Consider, without romanticizing, the work of the pre-Industrial Revolution farmer's wife. Yes, much was creative, and there was variation we lack today in housework. Of course, no one is stopping any woman from quilting or bread-making or sewing or cooking—to name a few of the creative venues of our foremothers. But who of us would really rather do our laundry by hand? Heat our irons on the stove top? Cook with wood? Sew *all* our clothing and linens (including underwear, jeans, sheets), without a sewing machine? Make our own lye soap? For myself, I remain thankful for many of the laborsaving devices we have and the convenience of many store-bought items.

A woman's work was hard and often thankless; it was simply expected of her, as was a man's. These women didn't get self-esteem from their economic contribution to the family; they got it from seeing their work as a form of *service* to their family. They were an important part of a valued social unit, accomplishing needed work and raising their children to understand *how* to work and *why* to work. My mother was no less so merely because she didn't do as much housework.

Women who were forced to work because of the less-beneficial effects of the Industrial Revolution still saw their work as service to the family, to help its survival as a valuable social unit. Today, for many women the motive to work for pay is entirely different. Their desire is to be *independent* of the family, to be *personally* fulfilled through the esteem of the world, rather than to serve others in what they call the "mundane" and "demeaning" work of homemaking and child-rearing.

How can women reduce homemaking and child-rearing to cleaning toilets and changing diapers? Whenever a feminist describes the work of a housewife and a mother, she uses the most boring, repetitive, and unglamourous examples to stand for the whole. I myself don't particularly care for dishwashing and housecleaning; but I do delight in a clean, friendly, and neat home to welcome both family and friends. And it's not changing diapers and wiping noses I dwell on from my children's early years. It's first smiles and first words and first steps; it's learning to share and to say "I'm sorry" and to throw a ball; it's laughing and crying and loving together. And this is what many women think they *wish* to give up for jobs that will certainly have their own share of drudgery, the fickle acclaim of the world, the stress of constant production for people to whom they are not indispensable and who can't possibly care about them as much as their own children do.

Perhaps the most deleterious effect of the Industrial Revolution is the splitting of the family unit as it used to exist. When families worked together to run a farm or a shop or a trade, *both* parents had much more interaction with the children, and the children learned more about the realities of work and responsibility than they do in today's culture, when so much time is spent with peers, and even activities like sports are becoming more and more self-centered and win-at-any-cost. Apparently a growing number of families agree with this assessment, as home-based businesses and telecommuting are on the rise, not always just women but spouses together working from home to be with their children and involve them in the business.

Homeschooling allows for a similar interaction with children. Even if it can't be combined with a home business, mothers can make sure their children get into the community and have greater and more meaningful social interactions than the graded school system allows for. Because children go with Mom everywhere (shopping, Bible studies, volunteer work, etc.), because they have a wide variety of contact with adults and children of all ages, they generally show greater maturity at younger ages, better ability to get along with others, and less reliance on peer approval in their decision-making.

Homeschooling isn't for everyone; home businesses aren't even legally possible everywhere. But families with children should at least explore the various options before automatically placing children in day care and government schools—especially if the reason is that the wife feels a "need" for a career to satisfy her own esteem. If a family decides that homeschooling isn't an option, for example, then a mother's time away from paid work may be only a few years before the children enter private or government schools for several hours each day. But every mother who *can* should seriously consider spending at a minimum the preschool years with her children and being available before and after school during the school years—for the welfare of her children.

Raymond and Dorothy Moore have many years of experience and research in early childhood education. *Better Late Than Early* presents their findings from an extensive review and integration of research from many scientific fields. Their thesis is: "During the first crucial eight years, home should be the child's only nest and parents the teachers for their children. These are the years when the child requires affection and emotional security more than learning skills, when he should be able to get ready for life unfettered by school rules" (3). All the studies they reviewed (several hundred for the more technical *School Can Wait*, which first presented their findings) suggest that children are not ready for formal learning in a school setting before they achieve an integration of various physical, emotional, and cognitive abilities (called the Integrative Maturity Level—IML), which generally occurs somewhere from ages eight to ten, even later for some children.

Reading, for example, is a far more complex skill than most people realize, dependent on such abilities as hearing the differences between sounds, visually distinguishing similarly shaped letters, reasoning logically from cause to effect, and making connections between new and previous information. Consistently, the research shows that those abilities are not sufficiently developed for true reading skills (comprehension and use of information, not mere decoding of words) until ages eight to ten. Earlier efforts to make children read often lead to nearsightedness, learning disabilities, and early discouragement with school as their days are marked with consistent failures. It is far better for children to begin maturing naturally through work and play in the family setting until they are ready for more formal education.

Homeschooling allows parents to teach reading and other cognitive skills as each child is ready, instead of assuming all children are alike. We had children learn to read at every age from an early four (the only one with eye problems) to a late eight—and all are excellent and avid readers today. In fact, this ability to take each child at his or her own pace—both for learning basic skills and getting through advanced subjects—is one of the most highly attractive features of homeschooling for most parents who choose it. Johnny can race ahead in math if it's easy for him, while taking a more average pace to understand some scientific concepts. His younger sister may outpace him in science but take longer to fully grasp the concept of division by fractions. All are held to high standards, but each can achieve those standards in his own best timing.

Socialization also benefits from a primarily home influence. Most day cares and preschools cannot offer a great deal of one-on-one attention to children; so they lack the adult model of appropriate behavior and the gentle insistence of a loving adult for obedience and respect. Study after study shows that children whose school entry is delayed until eight or later are the ones who have the highest levels of self-confidence and leadership ability—because self-discipline and respect for others were first developed in the nonthreatening environment of a loving family. Only when a child has developed a full sense of security within the home is he ready to step out into the bigger world and function readily within it instead of being intimidated by it.

Physical health (a child's immune system is not mature until eight or later) and language skills, as mentioned earlier, are other good reasons for a mother to be at home full-time during at least a child's first several years. If a family determines that private or government school is the best option at that time, a mother might still consider not returning to full-time work outside the home until her children are older. Schoolchildren benefit in many important ways from the availability of a parent before and after school. Simple physical danger increases when a child walks into an empty house, from criminal action against him to accidents that might require more than a Band-Aid. Temptations increase for the unsupervised child—maybe it would be more fun to go somewhere forbidden such as with a mischievous (or worse) friend or do something forbidden such as watching improper television shows or surfing the Internet for pornography sites. And the unsupervised child may simply feel less secure with no one to welcome him home, to hear about his day, maybe to alleviate some anxiety that he won't want to share later on. All of these problems, of course, may affect academic progress too.

During these school years, a mother may decide to work

part-time or work from the home or take classes toward a degree or certification and thus be available for her child before and after school. In my own case, although I didn't share many of my miserable experiences at school with my mother, just knowing that she would be at home and that I would be entering a safe place where I was valued and loved made me eager to be there and kept me from foolish choices I might otherwise have been more tempted to make.

Fathers, of course, are important in their children's lives as well as mothers, and too many give too little time. The complete absence of fathers can devastate children, as can the emotional absence of a physically present father. However, even those fathers who give as much time as possible to their children generally work outside the home, and thus the continual care devolves on the mother. In our family, I have been the primary wage earner and my husband the primary caregiver since our oldest was about seven. This seems a far better situation than day care; yet a father, however loving and conscientious, isn't a mother, and our children have expressed their missing my time and energy in their lives. They have learned wonderful skills from their dad, but they missed the more nurturing care of a mother. A home business would have been ideal for our family had we been able to pursue one, combining the different strengths of each parent throughout the day.

In considering our options when children are young and in school, it's good to remember that these years are only a part of our lives. All too soon the children will be grown and gone, and our options will change again. A mother may decide at that point to return to full-time work, or some may begin work outside the home for the first time. Others may choose to become more involved in community and church work or pursue creative work they've put on hold. Even in these choices, our vocation as mother should hold a place: How available do we wish to be to our grown children? What kind of grandmothers do we wish to be when their children enter our lives?

Returning to the example of the Proverbs 31 woman we looked at in the previous chapter, it's clear there's no biblical tradition that women aren't to work for wages. Even the instruction of Paul to Titus that the older women should teach the younger women to be "workers at home" (Titus 2:5, NASB) refers to home management and doesn't preclude paid work. The woman of Proverbs 31 made belts and garments and sold them. She bought real estate and planted vineyards. She was able to do this within the daily round of work in her home, however, which is harder for modern women.

At times someone remarks that laborsaving devices are the modern woman's servants. However, although they obviously cut down the time needed on a task, they are not quite the same. If I tell a servant to do the laundry, I can go about other tasks without concerning myself with that one. But with my handy washing machine, I still have to sort, load, and unload the clothes, hang out and bring them in, fold, iron, and put them away. Less time, yes—but not *no* time, and there is still a care on my mind. Extended families used to live together too, and an aunt or a grandmother might naturally take care of a child or finish a task while a mother worked out a bargain to sell her goods. These *are* different times.

Yet God doesn't leave us without guidance. The doctrine of vocation tells us that when a woman marries and has children, her primary responsibilities lie in being a wife and mother; these are the closest relationships to her, the people she has the greatest direct responsibility to and for. How can she best be her husband's helpmeet and raise her children to be competent, caring adults? All else comes within these parameters, but it may well be that God will direct her gifts in such a way that paid work from or outside the home becomes a part of her life without infringing on those first duties. Only in prayer and obedience to God and in harmony with her husband can these decisions be made. And we do well not to judge the decisions of others without knowledge of their motives and circumstances.

CHAPTER NINE

Women in the Church

§

Some of the early feminists wanted to see women admitted to leadership positions in the church, but this was never a major issue of the movement. The modern movement, secular as it is, has not been particularly concerned with women in the church either. However, Christian women who saw that the secular feminists had some good points to make began to explore how feminism and Christianity might fit together. We have discussed the result in Chapter 4: a feminism that claims that the equality of men and women before God also precludes any concept of gender-based leadership and submission; women thus should be able to function appropriately in any role in the church, including teaching and leadership. We also looked at why, based on the creation story and New Testament teaching, this view does not accord with the plain meaning of Scripture.

Christian women who call for leadership positions in the church have been influenced by the assumptions of secular feminists: namely, that there are no innate differences between men and women, that hierarchy necessarily equates to superiority and inferiority, and that the value of a person is best appraised by the prestige of his or her paid position in society—all questionable at best. But another, somewhat more legitimate basis for this call exists, and that is the not always positive experience of women in the church. Too often women's gifts have not been nurtured and directed into meaningful service in the church and community. Too often stereotypical assumptions about their interests have dictated the ways they are asked and expected to serve. Too often the needs of women in abusive or other difficult situations have not been met. Too often women have not been respected and affirmed, as women or as equals in Christ.

But need we throw out doctrine to rectify these problems? Today's secular feminists have "solved" the sexual double standard by making women more promiscuous instead of calling men to become more chaste—an obvious absurdity and most destructive to both individuals and society. But feminists in the church today are trying to solve the problems of women by embracing the same formula their secular counterparts embrace—making women more like men. Yet the answer cannot lie in the church becoming more like the world, in forcing Scripture to accord with the values of a secular, anti-Christian culture. Rather, we should boldly follow the clear teaching of Scripture, proclaiming the freedom it offers and showing the world that God's way is both different and far more satisfying.

The restrictions given women in the New Testament concerning teaching and holding authority over men are actually quite narrow. The context in every case is appropriate behavior in the public meetings of the church and in its overall administration. This would only restrict women from teaching the entire congregation and an adult class or Bible study including men, and from administrative positions of authority over men, such as that of elder as described in 1 Timothy and Titus. These restrictions are based on the creation order (Adam was given primary responsibility for the spiritual welfare of the family) and on the nature of the Fall (a reversal of the leadership and submission roles). Now God asks us to reaffirm the creation order in the public ministry of the church, out of obedience to Him and as a testimony to the world.

Only in obedience will we find contentment. Women have been increasingly abandoning the homemaker role for full-time, "challenging" careers in the marketplace, only to find that they feel they are missing out on the most important aspect of life—family. "Women today are no more satisfied than they were in the 50s," psychologist Mary Pipher asserted on an *ABC World News* broadcast (June 7, 2000), which also cited a study indicating that the majority of women would prefer to work part-time, not at all, or in volunteer positions if their families could afford it (Hayes). If it is true that even secular women are feeling a pull toward more time in nurturing and serving roles than in the spotlight of socially prestigious careers, then isn't it possible that nurturing and serving are the natural roles of women, that feminist demands for power and prestige are the results of fallen womanhood, and that Christian women should hold out a different, scriptural solution to women's problems, drawing their secular sisters to the church for answers that satisfy their thirst for significance?

To do this, however, means that many churches need to take seriously the restlessness and discontentment of their women, encourage and affirm their womanhood *and* their pursuit of all roles open to them, and offer ministries that honestly address the real harm caused both by the male tendency to dominate and the female tendency to control. Listening to women does not mean bowing to feminist distortions of truth. It takes discernment to sort out the real needs from their sometimes inaccurate articulation and the inappropriate solutions that are suggested. But to do this is essential if women in the church are to reach their potential, if they are to glorify God and love their neighbors as fully as He intends.

Women who say that the church is unfair to limit them from holding positions of authority have probably been hurt in some way by the disrespect or domination of men—perhaps merely the clear sense that men in the church don't value their gifts or suggest by their words or actions that women are inferior to men. These messages can be given so easily—a tone of voice, demeaning jokes, brushing off suggestions, etc., as well as through the over-restriction of women's roles. Then women often react by trying to prove they are "as good as men," by behaving *like* men to try to earn their respect.

Watching an episode of *JAG* one night, I was struck by the female lead's response to the man who was helping her prosecute a case. He suggested, rather forcefully, that she should let him present a particular argument because she was "too involved." She answered, "I finally convinced Harm [the male lead] that my emotions do not affect my decisions about my cases; I'll convince you, too." It's a telling episode in more than one way. When men insist on believing that women are inevitably *controlled* by their emotions and cannot think or act rationally, they stereotype in a demeaning and hurtful way. Yet when women entirely *repress* their emotions to prove the stereotype untrue, they repress an aspect of their femininity that could bring insights to bear that a man might be more likely to miss. Both are wrong. Since each of us has a sin nature, we must each rely on the Holy Spirit to teach us to act out our manhood or womanhood in godly, balanced ways. It is surely the church's responsibility to help us do so.

How can the church affirm women and womanhood? It could certainly begin by teaching what *both* biblical manhood and biblical womanhood are. It does seem that far too often in conservative churches a disparate emphasis is placed on the concept of submission. And while gender-segregated studies of manhood and womanhood are important, only with an understanding of both can we joyfully embrace our own vocation of gender or possibly understand how to respond in a godly manner to the distortion of that vocation in a spouse or others. Such studies must stress the equal value of men and women in God's eyes and the ways they have been designed to complement one another. Both manhood and womanhood should be celebrated as gifts of God to each of us for our contentment and joy in this life. Young people in particular need to hear this message often and clearly as they try to steer their way into adulthood while being constantly barraged with ungodly messages about sex and male and female roles.

The church must also acknowledge the very real consequences of the sins of men against women, as well as those of women against men. Only through an understanding of the biblical concepts of manhood and womanhood can truly helpful counsel be given to women who are being abused in various ways by the men in their lives; only through that understanding can women ensnared in sinful behavior be freed to become Christlike. It is encouraging to see more women counselors in church settings—*if* they are genuinely counseling scriptural truth and not merely offering the world's failures with a Christian veneer.

Finally, the church needs to actively encourage women to use their gifts in ministry both in the church and in the community. Rather than making assumptions about what women want to do or can do, we need to listen to individual women and direct them toward the best use of their particular gifts. I doubt there will ever be a dearth of women eager to serve in the "traditional" ways—nursery care, meals for the sick, etc. But many of us are not comfortable with these roles, though we may be more than glad to help now and then, and there are places for us also.

John Piper has drawn up a sample of types of ministries women might be part of, and Wayne Grudem has done similarly in an article titled "What *Should* Women Do in the Church?" Drawing on these, I will explore some of the possibilities for ministry by women. Realizing it is impossible to be comprehensive, the following is meant only to suggest the wide variety of ways—not replacing but expanding the "traditional"—that women can serve in and through the church.

One area of restricted service for women is the public meetings of the church, where we cannot teach or take an authoritative role. There remain, however, a number of ways we can participate besides sitting in the congregation. A musically talented woman may lead congregational or choir singing or be part of a music team. A woman might read Scripture, make announcements, lead in prayer, share a testimony, or talk about a ministry opportunity. If a church uses dramatic presentations, a woman could lead and/or participate in these. One of the most amazing and edifying worship times for me included a young woman's dance interpretation of an Easter song. Miriam would be an example of a woman who led the congregation in dramatic worship of the Lord after the crossing of the Red Sea.

What about prophesying in the public meetings? Stephen's daughters exercised this gift in New Testament times, and Paul refers to it. Views differ as to exactly what this gift entails. Some see it as one of the charismatic gifts. Others see it as the application of Scripture to particular circumstances, others as foretelling the future. First Corinthians 14:3 says, "He who prophesies speaks edification and exhortation and comfort to men," and verses 22-25 tell us prophecy is meant for the edification of believers but will convict unbelievers as well. Regardless of the exact content of prophecy, I want to look at what's definite about it and how it relates to women in particular.

First Corinthians 11 tells us prophecy is not forbidden to women in the public meetings, as Paul gives instruction on the decorum to be observed when they do. Because teaching men is explicitly denied in 1 Timothy 2, we can be confident that, whatever else it is, prophecy is not a *teaching* gift. First Corinthians 14:29-35 gives explicit instruction concerning the exercise of prophecy in the meetings. One prophet would speak at a time, and the others would judge, one by one. Since the instruction to women to "keep silent" immediately follows this, it appears that a woman might prophesy but could not judge the prophecies of others. Therefore, the judgment of prophecy must be a form of teaching; it would perhaps involve correcting or drawing out the content from Scripture. Thus any error a prophet, male or female, spoke would be immediately corrected by other— male—prophets. If a woman questioned what was said, and her question was not answered by the male prophets in their judgments, she was to ask her husband about it at home and not act unseemly by challenging another prophet publicly.

What this means for today's public meetings is not completely clear to me, as most of our services are quite different from the ones described here. Churches I am familiar with generally have a single teacher deliver an exegesis of Scripture, a teaching message. Evening services in some churches may be open for several people to share in a variety of ways, perhaps more nearly approximating what Paul refers to—though I've never heard anyone publicly correct anyone else in a church meeting! At the least, this passage would preclude a woman from doing just that, publicly questioning or correcting what someone else has shared if she believes him to be wrong. Instead, she should ask her husband about the issue at home, and if they agree that the teaching was incorrect, then it would be time to speak to someone in authority about it, in private.

The key, I believe, in this and all situations that raise questions about precise meaning, is our willingness, first, to defer to the authority of the local church, and second, to discuss such an issue privately with the church leadership if we believe Scripture is not being accurately understood or followed. When God gives gifts, it is also up to Him to present us with opportunities to use them, and if a particular opportunity is not available, perhaps we need to be open to other possibilities; His opportunities may not look as we expect them to. Certainly the gifts are given solely for the edification of the body and are not to cause needless divisions. (I am not here going to attempt to say what issues are important enough to break fellowship over; for that I commend each saint to his or her own conscience before the Lord.)

Women are also denied at least the office of elder as defined in 1 Timothy 3 and Titus 1: They are not to hold authority over men in the church. However, there are administrative positions women may be allowed to fill that would not involve the kind of authority given to an elder. Grudem has noted that there might well be some disagreement as to exactly where to draw the line in any of these areas. Some churches, for example, may believe a woman can hold a committee chairmanship or be their Christian Education Director, while others may believe these positions involve too much exercise of authority. More would agree that a woman could be a Sunday school superintendent, and it would seem logical for a woman to act as a coordinator of a church's women's ministries or as head of a particular women's ministry. Administrative assistant, secretary, treasurer, director of Vacation Bible School, coordinator of audiovisual services—all these kinds of ministries offer a woman who enjoys organization opportunities to be a part of church administration without overstepping biblical boundaries for her service. It's possible that Phoebe served the infant church in some sort of administrative way without wielding authority over men in the congregations.

Ministries to the saints abound with opportunities for service. For women gifted in teaching, many Sunday school levels are open: adult and college women's classes and mixed classes at lower levels, as well as home Bible studies for women. I don't think any of my teaching has brought greater satisfaction than the several weeks four of us spent poring over God's Word about marriage, getting to know each other, sharing our experiences, our fears, our victories, our failures, together growing closer to what God desires us to be as women. Titus 2:3-5 came alive for all of us. Teaching in Christian schools and colleges is also an opportunity to help young people grow in their walk with the Lord. Prayer ministries are ideal for women to be a part of; if time doesn't allow for coordinating and promoting such a ministry, we can always find time as we go about daily tasks to lift up the needs and praises of our brothers and sisters. This was apparently considered an especially powerful ministry for widows (1 Tim. 5:5).

Writing offers many opportunities for ministry to the saints too. From the local (writing and editing church materials) to the universal (writing books and articles, commentaries, Bible studies, Sunday school curriculum), women can be involved in the lives of believers in significant ways. How do some of these differ from teaching that is proscribed by Scripture? Grudem says of writing, "The teaching relationship of an author to a reader is much more like the one-to-one kind of teaching that Priscilla and Aquila did when they explained the way of God more clearly to Apollos in Acts 18:26. In fact, with a book the element of direct personal interaction is almost entirely absent. Moreover, the book comes not only from the author but also with input from the editors and publisher" (3). An author, in reality, has no authority over his or her audience; they are under no obligation to follow the author's teaching except as the Holy Spirit might convict them of truth through it. And the church is in dire need of writers who can articulate truth clearly and even eloquently.

Women in the church often find there are few places to go if they are in need of counseling help, either because they are uncomfortable discussing their problems with a man or they do not think a man can understand. I have seen too many instances of a male-female counseling relationship drawn into sexual sin as well, which makes me admire the commitment of many pastors never to counsel a woman alone. Yet this very commitment may keep some women from seeking counsel as the level of discomfort rises with the number of people involved. Therefore, women counselors are a tremendous need in churches today, women with a commitment to Scripture and a heart that yearns to draw their sisters into the blessings of obedience to God's Word.

Discipling, mentoring, visitation, hospitality can all be done effectively by women in the church. Youth sponsorship is another need; while it's my opinion that junior high and high school youth need a man to be in authority over them (partly because many youth lack a good male role model and partly because men have an easier time of controlling this age group), women need to be involved with the youth as well—to give the girls someone to look up to and imitate, to be available to them as they struggle with questions and problems inappropriate to discuss with an older man, and to help the boys remember that respect is due to females of any age!

Most churches have social/evangelistic ministries in the community, and women can and should play many roles in these. Crisis pregnancy centers need directors and volunteers and serve a desperate need even in small communities. The CPC director in my small town just returned from a trip to Romania to train women there in dealing with women who have crisis pregnancies, are being abused, and so on. What an opportunity—and how far from even her imagination when she was first drawn to the CPC ministry. Students from kindergarten through high school can use tutors, mentors, counselors. Sports ministries can draw all ages for fun and character development as well as presenting an opportunity to share the love of Christ. Drama ministries, food banks, homeless shelters, prison ministries—the needs are countless, and women can serve in any position from establishing and directing such ministries to giving a few hours of volunteer service. Causes that are both moral and political make good ministry opportunities as well. Anne Ryun (wife of track champion Jim Ryun) has given hours of her time to Kansans for Life and other pro-family and pro-decency causes in their home town of Lawrence, Kansas, while homeschooling their children. Her visibility no doubt helped Jim in his successful bid for a seat in the U.S. House of Representatives.

Teaching opportunities abound in community outreach too. Teaching literacy classes, English for immigrants and migrant workers, homemaking skills, employment skills are all ways to offer practical help to needy people and at the same time share the reason for our commitment to them. Women who enjoy technical work can be involved in radio, TV, and film ministries. And again, writing is a way to reach out to believers and unbelievers with books and articles based on scriptural truths, fiction that reveals a godly worldview, and journalism that is biased toward truth instead of falsehood. Those who work in "secular" jobs also have tremendous opportunities to stand for truth in their job performance as well as making friends of people who need what Christ can offer.

Foreign missions is another area of service to consider. Women have been taking the Gospel to other peoples on their own, as wives and as members of mission teams for centuries. Generally, of course, the greatest need is evangelism, accompanied by Bible translation. Obviously, any of the ministries already suggested are open for women in the mission field. From singles like Grace Aylward to married women like Betty Stam to widowed mothers like Elisabeth Elliot, women have courageously followed Christ's call to make disciples, placing love for Him above all human connections—and thus finding the human love God did provide that much sweeter.

A question inevitably arises with women missionaries and teaching: If they teach doctrine to men, as many of them must who are not married or part of a team of missionaries including men, are they not violating the Scriptures that say women cannot teach or have authority over men? There will no doubt be some less-than-ideal situations, and yet the story of Joanne Shetler suggests that a woman can teach for a time and still have a womanly attitude that encourages the men to begin taking responsibility for that task as soon as possible. Shetler, a Wycliffe missionary in the Philippines with the Balangao people, led the church meetings at first. Though she encouraged the men who had embraced the Lord to have an active part, they were at first reluctant—until they were helping her translate one of the passages requiring the silence of women. Upon hearing from Scripture that women were not to teach men in the public meetings, they themselves approached Shetler and requested that she teach them in private so they could lead, and after that took all public responsibility for the growing church—which had been her goal from the first and gave her cause for rejoicing in her role as a modern-day Priscilla.

No one, I think, would suggest that people should die without the opportunity to know Christ rather than allow a woman to explain Christian doctrine to them. Yet the scriptural example is always for men from within a congregation to become its pastors and teachers, and a woman missionary who has a proper regard for manhood will work toward that goal and will rejoice when it is understood and achieved. It would be obvious, however, that if a man is available—her husband or someone else on a missionary team—he should take the responsibility for public teaching and leadership until the native Christians are ready to take it over, so the people can see the appropriate relationship between men and women modeled from the first.

I have barely touched the surface of the ways women can serve the Lord. As Grudem points out, we need to be careful "not to prohibit what the Bible doesn't prohibit, while . . . attempting to preserve male leadership in a way Scripture directs" (7). It may well be appropriate for women to minister within the church and to the community and world in many ways we have tended to prohibit or discourage. If we will recognize this, then the church can affirm women and their gifts without placing them in positions of inappropriate authority and yet recognizing their equal and vital contributions to the church's twin purpose of building up believers and reaching out to unbelievers. God's glory can only increase as all saints use their gifts fully in His service.

There is, however, a broader context for the issue of who can—and can't—do what. Ultimately, we are called to *serve*, to serve God for His glory and man for his edification. Jesus, after washing the disciples' feet, said, "You call Me Teacher and Lord, and you say well, for so I am. If I then, your Lord and Teacher, have washed your feet, you also ought to wash one another's feet. For I have given you an example, that you should do as I have done to you. Most assuredly, I say to you, a servant is not greater than his master; nor is he who is sent greater than he who sent him. If you know these things, blessed are you if you do them" (John 13:13-17).

This example we are all called to follow, but especially men are called to self-sacrificial leadership in the home and church. Earlier we looked at the husband's leadership in the home; a look now at what is required of leaders in the church may prove helpful in understanding how they are to lead. Let me acknowledge that various terms are used to denote leadership positions in the church. The duties I discuss here may be ascribed to "elders," "bishops," "deacons," presbyters," "pastors," etc., depending on the denomination. For simplicity, as I summarize Paul's instructions to the men he left in charge of the churches in Ephesus and Crete, I have chosen to use the single term "elder." First and 2 Timothy and Titus contain Paul's instructions for church leaders, in which he integrates an elder's responsibilities to the body with his responsibilities in developing and guarding his own character. Although Paul moves back and forth between these responsibilities, I will separate them for a more convenient summary.

The duties of an elder, from these letters, appear to be divided basically between doctrine and administration. Paul instructs Timothy and Titus to teach the Word in various ways: read it in the meetings, preach, instruct, convince their listeners of its truth, affirm its truth. Along with teaching doctrine, they are to urge the believers to obey it, through commands, exhortations, rebukes, corrections, reminders. Both teaching and urging to obedience are to be done "with all authority" (Titus 2:15). Also, they are to shape their speech to those who listen—exhorting older men like fathers, older women like mothers, younger men and women like brothers and sisters. Church administration is suggested by Paul's instruction to Titus to appoint elders and to "set in order" whatever is lacking in a congregation (1:5). He also gives specific instructions to Timothy regarding how to honor the widows in their midst by determining who is to be supported by the church and who by relatives. The elders, then, have considerable authority in matters of doctrine and administration—one reason that a plurality of elders is wise, for they hold each other accountable; in fact, an elder who sins is to be publicly rebuked by the other elders (1 Tim. 5:20), thus preventing any one elder from abusing his authority.

This authority is to be exercised by men of godly character, and Paul gives far more attention to an elder's need to be above reproach and continually growing in his spiritual walk than he does to the exercise of authority. He tells both Timothy and Titus not to let the believers "despise" them, but the way they are to do this is by being examples of godliness themselves. They are to show the believers righteousness in word, conduct, love, spirit, faith, purity, and good works. They must "take heed to" themselves, pursuing righteousness, godliness, patience, gentleness, peace, humility. As young men, in particular they are to "flee also youthful lusts," and they mustn't let themselves be drawn into quarrels and foolish disputes and contentions.

Elders must expect afflictions, sufferings, and hardship and endure all these as "good soldiers" (see 2 Tim. 2:3). At all times they must continue in right doctrine—meditating on the Scriptures, giving themselves entirely to understanding and obedience, guarding the truth faithfully, handling the Word accurately, and showing in their teaching of doctrine "integrity, reverence, incorruptibility, sound speech that cannot be condemned" (Titus 2:7). Paul particularly exhorts Timothy to "stir up the gift of God which is in you" (2 Tim. 1:6) and to "fight the good fight" (1 Tim. 6:12).

The authority of elders comes only with a tremendous responsibility of personal holiness. Although they are to command and even rebuke the believers they shepherd, they earn the right to do so by their own blameless behavior, and they must always do so in humility and patience and long-suffering love, not lording it over anyone but laying down their own lives in obedience in order to draw others to a closer walk with the Lord Jesus Christ. And they will be held accountable before God for the lives of the believers in the church: "Obey those who rule over you, and be submissive, for they watch out for your souls, as those who must give account. Let them do so with joy and not with grief, for that would be unprofitable for you" (Heb. 13:17). James admonishes the believers that not many should become teachers because they "shall receive a stricter judgment" (James 3:1).

We see, then, that a leader is one who serves and yet retains the authority of leadership, just as Christ does in His relationship to the church. His sacrificial leadership is the example we are to follow; He gives us no example of "lording it over" those who are led. And His servant heart led Him not to the world's glory and honor but to the cross. Are we willing to be servants for His sake? Are we willing to acknowledge the leadership He has designed, in the home and the church, and not grasp for position ourselves? I wonder how many of us would want leadership positions if we truly understood the kind of sacrificial love that takes us to the cross for the sake of those we lead.

I do not hear the feminists within the church crying out for more positions of obvious service; I hear them crying out for positions of leadership and authority—because, they say, the men have all the power and prestige and good pay. Perhaps the greatest fault of the church lies here—in the worldly sort of "leadership" that makes others envious. If more of our leaders, in the church and in the home, would exemplify for us the true sacrificial leadership Paul describes, it could make it easier for others not to feel left out or unvalued. Instead, we would honor them for the sacrifices they make and not for the power they wield, and we would not be so anxious for the positions that demand such high sacrifice.

Regardless, though, of what others may do, God has clearly called women to a special vocation that emphasizes nurturing service. If we embrace the way He created us, we can serve gladly anywhere and draw others to us to learn about—and perhaps find—the Source of our joy and contentment. That is the ultimate purpose of our entire existence: to glorify God and draw others to Him. We women have a unique way to accomplish that purpose. May we stop grasping at the world's baubles and enjoy the true treasure that is already ours.

CHAPTER TEN

Let Your Light Shine

ꕥ

Hear the call of God to be a woman. Obey that call.
Turn your energies to service. . . . [Then] you will
know fullness of life, fullness of liberty, and
(I know whereof I speak) fullness of joy.
—ELISABETH ELLIOT TO HER DAUGHTER, VALERIE

When my older daughter married last summer, I wanted her to understand what it means to be a godly woman in a world that values self above all and rejects the wisdom of the One who created us to serve. The letter I wrote her seems a fitting close to this book, a challenge to us all to live joyfully in the gift of womanhood He has bestowed, trusting Him for the desires of our hearts.

Dear Davina,

You have been married one week today, and you and Val are enjoying the last days of your honeymoon. How beautiful you looked walking down the aisle to meet him, your face radiant with the joy of that special moment. The emotional high of that day can't last forever, but I pray that the radiance of your commitment remains even in the difficult times that are sure to come.

You have said that you desire to have a Christian marriage, to be a Christian wife. I am thankful for this desire—and I know, too, that it means your way will sometimes be lonely and difficult and confusing because you live in a world where the greatest goods are autonomy and the instant gratification of material and sensual desires. The only real advice I can give you is to trust your Lord and lean on Him moment by moment for His wisdom, not relying on your mere human reasoning.

The world tells you to look out first for yourself—get a better job where you can advance, make a name for yourself, pursue prestige and wealth, make enough money to contribute at least half of the household finances (and have something to fall back on if the marriage fails), above all be beholden to Val for nothing, be completely autonomous, your own person.

But God has given you a different perspective. Whatever job you may hold until children come, whether you complete your college degree or not, you know that you have never been and will never be your "own" person. In the moment of commitment, you and Val became one for life—not in your personalities or your feelings and opinions or your ways of thinking, but in the mysterious way you were already one with Christ, who makes us more ourselves while making us more like Himself. This is a paradox, this becoming one with another person, putting him and his needs and desires above your own, yet becoming more fully yourself in the process.

Gerard Manley Hopkins wrote of the "inscape" of every created thing, its uniqueness in its creation by God: "*myself* it speaks and spells, / Crying *what I do is me: for that I came.*" At the same time that we are utterly unique, we who love Christ also show forth Christ. The saint "Acts in God's eye what in God's eye he is—/ Christ. For Christ plays in ten thousand places, / Lovely in limbs and lovely in eyes not his / To the Father through the features of men's faces" (II. 7-8, 11-14).

And so you are unique and yet one with your Lord and one with your husband. Be careful, sweetheart, never to confuse the two with whom you are one; because Val is *there*, physically present, and you love him and rely on him so deeply, it can be a very real temptation. Remember when you feel that Val has failed you (sometimes he will, and sometimes you will only think he has) the warning of Oswald Chambers: "If we love a human being and do not love God"—or put the person we love above God—"we demand of him every perfection and every rectitude, and when we do not get it we become cruel and vindictive; we are demanding of a human being that which he or she cannot give. There is only one Being Who can satisfy the last aching abyss of the human heart, and that is the Lord Jesus Christ. . . . He knows that every relationship not based on loyalty to Himself will end in disaster" (July 30).

I know that you understand this, and I believe that you are learning it day by day, but marriage will challenge you to practice it yet more fully, at times when it will be more difficult than ever. When you are determined and Val is unreasonable (or seems so to you), when he says the hurtful thing or neglects the kind word, when you are tired and depressed and he is full of fun and happiness or the other way around—these times and more will tempt you to forget that he is but human, as are you, and there is only One who understands always and meets our exact needs always, allowing us to repent and forgive, whichever is necessary (often both), and still love.

Chambers also says, "The main thing about Christianity is not the work we do, but the relationship we maintain [with Christ] and the atmosphere produced by that relationship" (August 4). Remember this when you or others are tempted to define you primarily by some role you play, whether that of wife and (someday) mother, or student, or wage earner. These roles are not unimportant, and you must fulfill each with care, but they do not define you; your relationship to your Lord defines you.

And that relationship offers you the opportunity to live as a shining light in this darkened culture. What a privilege to represent your Lord—by His power, not your own—as His daughter in a culture crying out for direction, for truth. Never see this as a burden imposed on you, but as a gift of the highest order, to be cherished above all other gifts. Exercise it daily, so that it becomes an unconscious part of all you are and do.

To be a light . . .

Jesus says, "Let your light so shine before men, that they may see your good works and glorify your Father in heaven" (Matt. 5:16). The most important question you may ever answer as a Christian woman is this: How will you distinguish yourself in your journey through life so that others are drawn, not to you, but to the One who lights your soul? (And I have seen His light in your soul; you grow daily more beautiful in your love for Him.)

Remember the story of the moth that appears in Annie Dillard's *Holy the Firm*? A moth flew into the candle by which Dillard was reading while on a camping trip, "frazzled and fried in a second," leaving only "the glowing horn shell of her abdomen and thorax—a fraying, partially collapsed gold tube jammed upright in the candle's round pool." But this shell acted as a second wick, drawing fire through it, "glowing within, like a building fire glimpsed through silhouetted walls, like a hollow saint, like a flame-faced virgin gone to God, while I read by her light, kindled . . . while night pooled wetly at my feet" (17).

God asks of us nothing less than this complete sacrifice if we are to be lights in the world—nothing left of the self but a shell for the channeling of His glory. "Whoever desires to save his life will lose it, but whoever loses his life for My sake will find it" (Matt. 16:25). You will become more and more the woman God means you to be as you make this complete sacrifice, lose yourself, die to the old nature that desires recognition and approval, and let God have His way with you.

Madeleine L'Engle says we do not seek death of the self to "be freed from the intolerable wheel of life," as the Eastern mystics seek it. "No. We move—are moved—into death in order to be discovered, to be loved into truer life by our Maker" (*Walking*, 194). And this "truer life" is to be spent not for ourselves but for Him and for our neighbors.

And you spend this life uniquely as a woman.

Elisabeth Elliot, whose life shines as an example of someone unafraid to live and love, writes to her daughter, Valerie, "Womanhood is a call. It is a vocation to which we respond under God . . . thankful . . . for all that it means in a much wider sense [than mere marriage and motherhood], that in which every woman, married or single, fruitful or barren, may participate— the unconditional response exemplified for all time in Mary the virgin, and the willingness to enter into suffering, to receive, to carry, to give life, to nurture and to care for others" (*Let Me*, 62).

It is this gift, this vocation, of womanhood that allows you to be wife and someday mother, and that makes you love not only Val but your sister and your brothers, your friends and your colleagues in the special way you do—desiring their best, willing to sacrifice your time and your emotions to try to bring good to them. And it is the special sensitivity of your womanhood that sometimes makes it so hard; it is the sinful desire to control their responses that sometimes gets in the way of the selflessness you hope to act upon.

You are so like me, Davina! I know you have struggled with

this, have tried to make yourself not care because the pain of rejection or failure is so intense and because your greatest efforts sometimes seem to bear the least fruit. But like me, you have been unable to deny the gifts given you: the love of Christ Himself who agonized over you, the nurturing essence of your womanhood that must be expressed toward others, the artistic temperament that must experience the depths and the heights in order to create.

L'Engle shares a definition of *agape* from a book by Edward Nason West: It is "a profound concern for the welfare of another without any desire to control that other, to be thanked by that other, or to enjoy the process" (quoted in *Circle*, 158-159). This hits at the sinful desire we have to demand results of our loving as well as the depth of our righteous desire for the good of those we love. Only God can rid us of the desire to control, to be recognized, to find love easy. I see that He has begun this work in you, and what a joy—it took me so much longer to understand.

Something that helped me along the way was the understanding of God's desire for obedience. For so long my perfectionism (another trait you share with me) made me feel like a failure because nothing—from an embroidery project to raising a child—seemed to ever turn out the way it should have, the way I'd envisioned it. Then Lynn Ferguson (you will remember the loveliness of his wife, Patsy) shared at a Bible study that God is not interested so much in the results of what we do as in the process of our obedience. So much more than our paltry actions influence their results, and ultimately only God brings fruit in anyone's life. But He desires our simple obedience, by faith, step by step, knowing that He is the One who is ultimately able to work good through our lives if we only let Him live in and through us.

Psalm 144:12 says, "That our daughters may be as pillars,

sculptured in palace style." Elliot points out that the function of pillars is to support. This is the place God has designed for us women, the place of support, and it should be an encouragement to us to understand God's design: "We know that we fit into God's universe, we know our relation to the rest of mankind, to the family, and, if we have one, to a husband" (*Let Me*, 63-64). "Sculptured in palace style": The palace couldn't stand without us, but God is not merely utilitarian; its beauty is also enhanced by His design and our acceptance of it.

Sometimes this gift of womanhood, this desire to nurture and love, will seem too much, too overwhelming. Perhaps there will be tension between you and Val, a child in rebellion, a relative in trouble, a friend in need, expectations that wear you down. Remember in those moments the priorities given you by your primary vocation. Place your relationship with Val before all other earthly relationships, seek his good first, and give the rest to your Lord, who will give you the strength to do what He desires and the freedom to let all else go in peace. "We are all asked to do more than we can do," L'Engle reminds us (*Walking*, 61). This is what drives us to reliance on God; but never does He command what He does not provide the means and the strength to do.

Sometimes you will feel helpless in the face of the wretchedness you see all about you—friends hurting each other and themselves, divorce, violence, disease, despair . . . Again, what does God call you to do? Not to fix it all, or any of it—only He can fix the world's ills—but to begin with your family and move outward as He allows and directs, to do the "single acts of love" that may seem so small yet make all the difference in another's life. L'Engle says of these single acts: "They are all I have to give, and I am just falling prey to thinking that I can—or ought—to [fix the world] myself, if I under-estimate them" (*Circle*, 182).

To be a light means that others will look to you for guidance. And sometimes you will fail them, say the wrong thing, say nothing, act in the flesh instead of the Spirit. But failure is part of being human; perfection will not come until we are in heaven. And sometimes others will misunderstand and malign the light you bring, just as they did the Lord you serve. Never let your failures or the failures of others stop you from caring, from giving of the gifts God has blessed you with. As you grow in loving service to your Lord, you will understand that He brings good even from sin and failure, and that He never fails to pick us up and place us back on the right path, asking only that we try and repent and try again.

And when you succeed, He will give you yet more responsibility. Remember Shasta in C. S. Lewis's *The Horse and His Boy*, who discovered that the reward for one good deed is to be given another, yet more difficult and seemingly impossible. But your Lord is always with you, even in the fog of adversity or uncertainty or doubt.

And now your life is lived in a wonderful partnership with the friend who chose you for marriage; you have Val to share your burdens with and can trust in his wisdom to help you face them. Know, too, that as your nurturing, supportive, respectful love for him encourages him to lead, you will find more and more delight in following. Elliot describes the partnership of marriage as a dance: "It is the woman's delighted yielding to the man's lead that gives him freedom. It is the man's willingness to take the lead that gives her freedom. Acceptance of their respective positions frees them both and whirls them into joy" (*Let Me*, 185).

You *are* a light in this dark world, Davina. "You did not choose Me," our Lord says, "but I chose you, and appointed you that you should go and bear fruit" (John 15:16). It is up to you how brightly you will allow your light to shine, and up to Him to keep it burning—as He has already shown He will, through some moments darker than we either care to remember. You have accepted His choice. Living it by His power will be more exciting than any adventure you could imagine, more fulfilling than any life you could create for yourself, more truly good to Val, the children you will have, and the friends and neighbors who surround you than any plans your own heart could devise.

"To be a witness," Cardinal Suhard says, ". . . means to live in such a way that one's life would not make sense if God did not exist" (quoted in L'Engle, *Walking*, 31). Live in the joy of His call and in the blessing of His gifts—salvation, womanhood, marriage, family, friendship. May His blessings be rich along the way, and may your obedience as richly bless those you love.

Love always,
Mom
July 28, 2000

Works Cited

Anthony, Susan B. "Social Purity." Ida Husted Harper. *The Life and Work of Susan B. Anthony,* II. Indianapolis, 1898. 1004-1012. Reprinted in *Up from the Pedestal: Selected Writings in the History of American Feminism.* Ed. Aileen S. Kraditor. Chicago: Quadrangle, 1968. 159-167.

Aspy, Catherine. "Should Women Go into Combat?" *Reader's Digest.* February 2001. http://www.readersdigest.com/rdmagazine/specfeat/archives/shouldwomengointocombat.htm

Austen, Jane. *Pride and Prejudice.* London: Dent, 1963.

Ayers, David J. "The Inevitability of Failure: The Assumptions and Implementations of Modern Feminism." *Recovering Biblical Manhood and Womanhood: A Response to Evangelical Feminism.* Eds. John Piper and Wayne Grudem. Wheaton, IL: Crossway Books, 1991. 312-331.

Beadles, Nicholas Aston II. "Stewardship-Leadership: A Biblical Refinement of Servant-Leadership." *The Journal of Biblical Integration in Business.* Vol. 6 Fall 2000. 25-37.

Blackwell, Antoinette Brown. "Relation of Woman's Work in the Household to the Work Outside." *Papers and Letters at the First Woman's Congress of the Association for the Advancement of Woman.* New York, October 1873. Reprinted in *Up from the Pedestal: Selected Writings in the History of American Feminism.* Ed. Aileen S. Kraditor. Chicago: Quadrangle, 1968. 150-159.

Brownson, Orestes A. "The Woman Question." *The Works of Orestes A. Brownson* XVIII. Ed. Henry F. Brownson. Detroit, 1885. 388-389, 403. Reprinted in *Up from the Pedestal: Selected Writings in the History of American Feminism.* Ed. Aileen S. Kraditor. Chicago: Quadrangle, 1968. 192-194.

Chambers, Oswald. *My Utmost for His Highest.* New York: Dodd, 1935.

Chervin, Ronda. *Feminine, Free and Faithful.* San Francisco: Ignatius, 1986.

Christen, Yves. "Sex Differences in the Human Brain." *Gender Sanity.* Ed. Nicholas Davidson. Lanham, MD: UP of America, 1989. 146-161.

Cleveland, Grover. "Would Woman Suffrage Be Unwise?" *Ladies' Home Journal.* XXII. October 1905. 7-8. Reprinted in *Up from the Pedestal: Selected Writings in the History of American Feminism.* Ed. Aileen S. Kraditor. Chicago: Quadrangle, 1968. 199-203.

"Debate at Woman's Rights Convention." Fifth Annual Woman's Rights Convention, October 1854, Philadelphia. *History of Woman Suffrage.* I. 379-383. Reprinted in *Up from the Pedestal: Selected Writings in the*

History of American Feminism. Ed. Aileen S. Kraditor. Chicago: Quadrangle, 1968. 108-113.

Dew, Thomas R. "Dissertation on the Characteristic Differences Between the Sexes." *Southern Literary Messenger*. I. Richmond, 1835. 493-512. Reprinted in *Up from the Pedestal: Selected Writings in the History of American Feminism*. Ed. Aileen S. Kraditor. Chicago: Quadrangle, 1968. 45-47.

Dillard, Annie. *Holy the Firm*. New York: Harper, 1977.

Elliot, Elisabeth. *Let Me Be a Woman: Notes on Womanhood for Valerie*. Wheaton, IL: Tyndale, 1976.

———. "The Essence of Femininity: A Personal Perspective." *Recovering Biblical Manhood and Womanhood: A Response to Evangelical Feminism*. Eds. John Piper and Wayne Grudem. Wheaton, IL: Crossway Books, 1991. 394-399.

Friedan, Betty. *The Feminine Mystique*. New York: Dell, 1983.

Gage, Joslyn Matilda. "Address at a Convention." National Woman Suffrage Association in Washington. 1884. *History of Woman Suffrage*. IV. 28-30. Reprinted in *Up from the Pedestal: Selected Writings in the History of American Feminism*. Ed. Aileen S. Kraditor. Chicago: Quadrangle, 1968. 137-140.

Goldberg, Steven. "The Universality of Patriarchy." *Gender Sanity*. Ed. Nicholas Davidson. Lanham, MD: UP of America, 1989. 129-145.

Grimke, Angelina Emily. *Letters to Catherine E. Beecher, in Reply to an Essay on Slavery and Abolitionism, Addressed to A. E. Grimke*. Boston, 1838. Reprinted in *Up from the Pedestal: Selected Writings in the History of American Feminism*. Ed. Aileen S. Kraditor. Chicago: Quadrangle, 1968. 58-66.

Grudem, Wayne. "But What *Should* Women Do in the Church?" *CBMW News*. November 1995. Vol. 1, No. 2. 1, 3-7.

Hayes, Erin. *ABC World News*. June 7, 2000.

Hitchcock, James. "The Fall of Ozzie and Harriet: What Went Wrong in the Fifties." *Crisis*. November 1992. 15-19.

Hopkins, Gerard Manley. "As kingfishers catch fire." *Victorian Literature: Poetry*. Eds. Donald J. Gray and G. B. Tennyson. New York: Macmillan, 1976. 724.

Hunt, Harriot K. "Tax Protest." *History of Woman Suffrage*. I. 259-260. Reprinted in *Up from the Pedestal: Selected Writings in the History of American Feminism*. Ed. Aileen S. Kraditor. Chicago: Quadrangle, 1968. 228-230.

Johnson, Gregg. "The Biological Basis for Gender-Specific Behavior." *Recovering Biblical Manhood and Womanhood: A Response to*

Evangelical Feminism. Eds. John Piper and Wayne Grudem. Wheaton, IL: Crossway Books, 1991. 280-293.

Kassian, Mary A. *The Feminist Gospel: The Movement to Unite Feminism with the Church.* Wheaton, IL: Crossway Books, 1992.

——. *Women, Creation, and the Fall.* Wheaton, IL: Crossway Books, 1990.

Kellog, Abraham L. "Remarks of Abraham L. Kellog in New York State Constitutional Convention." *Revised Record of the Constitutional Convention of the State of New York.* 8 May 1894—29 September 1894. II. Albany, 1900. 433-436. Reprinted in *Up from the Pedestal: Selected Writings in the History of American Feminism.* Ed. Aileen S. Kraditor. Chicago: Quadrangle, 1968. 196-199.

Kraditor, Aileen S., ed. *Up from the Pedestal: Selected Writings in the History of American Feminism.* Chicago: Quadrangle, 1968.

L'Engle, Madeleine. *A Circle of Quiet.* San Francisco: Harper, 1972.

——. *Walking on Water: Reflections on Faith and Art.* New York: Farrar, Straus and Giroux, 1980.

Loveless, Cheri. "The Invisible Majority: America's Homemakers." *Gender Sanity.* Ed. Nicholas Davidson. Lanham, MD: UP of America, 1989. 177-186.

Mathewes-Green, Frederica. "Warning: The '50s Led to the '60s." *World Magazine.* January 22, 1994. 30.

——. "Let God be God." *World Magazine.* January 29, 1994. 30.

Moo, Douglas. "What Does It Mean Not to Teach or Have Authority over Men?" *Recovering Biblical Manhood and Womanhood: A Response to Evangelical Feminism.* Eds. John Piper and Wayne Grudem. Wheaton, IL: Crossway Books, 1991. 179-193.

Moore, Raymond S. and Dorothy N. Moore. *Better Late Than Early: A New Approach to Your Child's Education.* Washougal: Reader's Digest, 1986.

Morse, Anne. "Modem Mamas." *Citizen Magazine.* January 1999. Vol. 13, No. 1. 20-21.

Murray, Judith Sargent Stevens. "On the Equality of the Sexes." *Massachusetts Magazine.* II. March 1790. 132-135; and II. April 1790. 223-226. Reprinted in *Up from the Pedestal: Selected Writings in the History of American Feminism.* Ed. Aileen S. Kraditor. Chicago: Quadrangle, 1968. 30-39.

National Center for Educational Statistics. U.S. Government. http://www.nces.ed.gov

Palau, Luis. *Where Is God When Bad Things Happen?: Finding Solace in Times of Trouble.* New York: Doubleday, 1999.

Piper, John. "A Vision of Biblical Complementarity: Manhood and Womanhood Defined According to the Bible." *Recovering Biblical*

Manhood and Womanhood: A Response to Evangelical Feminism. Eds. John Piper and Wayne Grudem. Wheaton, IL: Crossway Books, 1991. 31-59.

Raphael, Rebecca. "Nine Weeks of Hell." *ABC News 2020 Downtown.* November/December 2000. http://www.abcnews.go.com/onair/2020/ 2020Downtown_001127_basictraining_feature.html

"Resolutions Passed at a Woman's Rights Convention." Worcester, 1851. *History of Woman Suffrage* I. 825-826. Reprinted in *Up from the Pedestal: Selected Writings in the History of American Feminism.* Ed. Aileen S. Kraditor. Chicago: Quadrangle, 1968. 220-222.

Rhodes, Ron. "The Debate over Feminist Theology: Which View is Biblical?" Reasoning from the Scriptures Ministry. http://home.earthlink.net/~ron-rhodes/Feminism.html

Rose, Ernestine. "On Legal Discrimination." *History of Woman Suffrage* I. 237-241. Reprinted in *Up from the Pedestal: Selected Writings in the History of American Feminism.* Ed. Aileen S. Kraditor. Chicago: Quadrangle, 1968. 222-228.

Sayers, Dorothy. "The Human-Not-Quite-Human." *Masculine/Feminine: Readings in Sexual Mythology and the Liberation of Women.* Eds. Betty Roszak and Theodore Roszak. New York: Harper, 1969. 116-132. Reprinted from *Unpopular Opinions.* New York, Harcourt, 1947. 142-149.

Shalit, Wendy. *A Return to Modesty: Discovering the Lost Virtue.* New York: The Free Press, 1999.

Stanton, Elizabeth Cady. "The Matriarchate, or Mother-Age." *Transactions of the National Council of Women of the United States.* Philadelphia, 1891: 218-227. Reprinted in *Up from the Pedestal: Selected Writings in the History of American Feminism.* Ed. Aileen S. Kraditor. Chicago: Quadrangle, 1968. 140-147.

Sommers, Christina Hoff. *The War Against Boys: How Misguided Feminism Is Harming Our Young Men.* New York: Simon & Schuster, 2000.

———. *Who Stole Feminism?: How Women Have Betrayed Women.* New York: Simon & Schuster, 1994.

Stearns, Jonathon F. "Discourse on Female Influence." *Female Influence, and the True Christian Mode of Its Exercise: A Discourse Delivered in the First Presbyterian Church in Newburyport.* July 30, 1837. Reprinted in *Up from the Pedestal: Selected Writings in the History of American Feminism.* Ed. Aileen S. Kraditor. Chicago: Quadrangle, 1968. 47-50.

"The Woman's Rights Convention—The Last Act of the Drama." Editorial, *New York Herald* September 12, 1852. *History of Woman's Suffrage* I. 853-854. Reprinted in *Up from the Pedestal: Selected Writings in the*

History of American Feminism. Ed. Aileen S. Kraditor. Chicago: Quadrangle, 1968. 189-191.

Thomas, M. Carey. "Present Tendencies in Women's College and University Education." *Publications of Collegiate Alumnae.* Series III, No. 17. February 1908. 45-50. Reprinted in *Up from the Pedestal: Selected Writings in the History of American Feminism.* Ed. Aileen S. Kraditor. Chicago: Quadrangle, 1968. 89-98.

Toynbee, Arnold. *The Industrial Revolution.* Gloucester, MA: Peter Smith, 1980.

Van Leeuwen, Mary Stewart. *Gender and Grace.* Downers Grove, IL: InterVarsity Press, 1990.

Vest, George G. "Remarks of Senator George G. Vest in Congress." *Congressional Record*, 49th Congress, 2nd Session, 25 January 1887. 986. Reprinted in *Up from the Pedestal: Selected Writings in the History of American Feminism.* Ed. Aileen S. Kraditor. Chicago: Quadrangle, 1968. 194-196.

Vincent, Lynn. "Worse NOW Than Ever." *World Magazine.* July 24, 1999. 14-18.

Webb, James. "Women Can't Fight." *Gender Sanity.* Ed. Nicholas Davidson. Lanham, MD: UP of America, 1989. 208-223.

Wingren, Gustaf. *Luther on Vocation.* Trans. Carl C. Rasmussen. Reprinted Evansville: Ballast Press, 1999.

Wollstonecraft, Mary. *A Vindication of the Rights of Women.* 2nd ed. Ed. Carol H. Poston. New York: Norton, 1988.

Index